Shashi Deshpande's *That Long Silence*

Critical Studies

Edited by
A.N. Dwivedi

Published by
ATLANTIC
PUBLISHERS & DISTRIBUTORS (P) LTD
7/22, Ansari Road, Darya Ganj, New Delhi-110002
Phones : +91-11-40775252, 40775214, 23273880, 23275880
Fax: +91-11-23285873
Web: www.atlanticbooks.com
E-mail: orders@atlanticbooks.com

Reprint, 2023

Printed & bound in India by Atlantic Print Services

Contents

Introduction .... *v*

Contributors .... *xi*

1. 'Writing of Us' in *That Long Silence* 1
Sanjoy Saksena

2. Defamiliarization of Self-Script in Shashi Deshpande's *That Long Silence* 21
Ashok Kumar Sharma

3. "Telling the Other Side of the Story" in Shashi Deshpande's *That Long Silence* 30
Veena Dwivedi

4. Breaking the Barriers: A Study of Shashi Deshpande's *That Long Silence* 45
Sanjana Shamshery

5. Breaking That Long Silence: The Quest for Space, Identity and Independence 65
Sthitaprajna

6. Emancipating the Bonded Self: A Study of Shashi Deshpande's *That Long Silence* 78
Monika Mathur

7. Deconstructing, Reconstructing Identities: Shashi Deshpande's *That Long Silence* 98
Minakshi Lahkar

8. Shashi Deshpande's *That Long Silence*: A Critique 108
Roopali

Appendices

Appendix 'A': The Dilemma of the Woman Writer 116
Shashi Deshpande

Appendix 'B': The Shorter Fiction of Shashi Deshpande: Search for Self 120
A.N. Dwivedi

Appendix 'C': Recurring Metaphors in Shashi Deshpande's Novels 129
A.N. Dwivedi

Index 141

Introduction

Shashi Deshpande is one of the leading Indian English novelists of today. Her persistence with the theme of 'Woman Question' in her novels and short stories occasionally raises doubts in our minds that she has taken sides with the problems of womankind, pushing the other half into the subordinate role, but this is far from the truth. She is not an aggressive feminist—quite unlike Lord Tennyson's princess who set up an academy solely for women, having barred the male entry strictly—who wants to live in an isolated tower, having no truck with the male world. Deshpande knows it well that this kind of existence is not possible in the real world, and that man and woman are the two equally important wheels of the chariot of life. Her attitude is, therefore, a balanced one, and does not create any fissure or fragmentation in man-woman relationship. And it is clearly reflected in her fictional writings.

I

That Long Silence (1988) is precisely a novel of this nature. Divided into four parts and carrying the Author's Note, the novel under review has raised the 'Woman Question' squarely and deals with the bitter-sweet life-story of Jaya and Mohan in their married relationship. At the beginning of the novel, the narrator (Jaya) says, "I'm writing of us. Of Mohan and me.... Self-revelation is a cruel process" (1). Jaya and Mohan lead a dull and monotonous life in a Dadar flat with their two children named Rahul and Rati. They live with the illusion of happiness, punctuated by dreary quarrels. Jaya is an educated woman, with a flair for writing, but on the objection of her husband she gives it up. She feels throttled and estranged from him. They are compared to "a pair of bullocks yoked together" (7). In an insightful article, Adle King calls the uneasy couple "odd misfits" involved in "petty bickerings over money" and "jealousy over affections" (1990: 165-66).

Jaya's relationship with Mohan becomes very bitter when in a mood of anger, she speaks of his mother 'a cook' (and this is a truth). Hearing this unexpected outburst from his educated wife, Mohan is upset and he stops speaking to her. He thinks that anger does not behove a woman and that it makes "a woman 'unwomanly'" (83). He observes a 'long silence' and maintains a distance from her. As in some other novels of Shashi Deshpande—*The Dark Holds No Terrors* (1980), *Roots and Shadows* (1983), and *The Binding Vine* (1993)—here too 'silence' becomes a recurring metaphor (as shown in my paper appended at the end of this book). This metaphor is so persistent in *That Long Silence* that it appears about half-a-dozen times in this novel. Silence signifies lack of communication, freezing of feeling, and want of understanding. The strain in conjugal relationship leads to the loss of identity, individuality and "personal vision" (147) on the part of Jaya. Also, because of this friction in personal relations, Jaya fails in her creative writings, precisely in her short stories. She is not happy with the change of her name from Jaya to Suhasini by her husband.

Jaya seeks solace in the company of Kamat, with whom she discusses her personal problems arising from the indifference of Mohan towards his family and children. Mohan suddenly slips away to Delhi, without letting anyone know about his whereabouts. Kamat consoles Jaya, like Bhaskar doing the same to Urmi in the *Binding Vine*, at this critical moment. They draw closer to each other and even start making physical advances. But unexpectedly, Kamat dies, leaving Jaya lonely and deserted. Jaya now decides to cut the ice and break the barriers of 'silence' on Mohan's return from Delhi. She is fed up with her marooned life, and the only way to come out of it, or to "erase the silence" (192) between Mohan and herself, is to speak to him and to listen to him. That indicates the change of attitude or the change of mind between the two. Both Jaya and Mohan come to realize that life cannot go on without the support of life-partners.

This is where the novel ends, on a note of hope and promise: "But we can always hope. Without that, life would be impossible. And if there is anything I know now, it is this: life has always to be made possible", says Jaya (193).

II

Here, in this collection of critical essays, *That Long Silence* is minutely studied by different scholars. The thrust area is 'the Woman Question', or still better, man-woman relationship in the fast-changing human world of our day. *That Long Silence* is a very popular novel of Shashi Deshpande, and it won the prestigious Sahitya Akademi Award for her in 1989. After that, Shashi Deshpande was offered the coveted Padmashri Award. This novel is prescribed in Indian and foreign universities, and hence its increasing demand day by day.

Apart from the editor's brief note on *That Long Silence* in the form of Introduction, this collection contains seven papers on this novel by as many hands as well as three appendices. The first paper, "'Writings of Us' in *That Long Silence*", by Sanjoy Saksena points out that Jaya's feminist role in the novel is both self-protective and subversive, and that it is a part of her domestic politics. Her silence serves as a shield for her as well as a self-evolved device against assertive Mohan. After a good deal of tension between the couple, good sense dawns upon Jaya and Mohan to come closer to each other in a spirit of understanding and to break the long-drawn silence. The telegram from Mohan—that all is well—reinforces the conjugal bond between them and puts them on the right track. Jaya's imagination starts working and brings in hope and relief for the family.

The second paper, "Defamiliarization of Self-Script in Shashi Deshpande's *That Long Silence*", by Ashok Kumar Sharma suggests that *That Long Silence* may be a part of Deshpande's past life, but it is not her autobiography. The novel may have self-reflections in certain episodes and through certain characters, but such reflections can't be connected to the life-story of the artist. What the paper emphasizes is that the reader should approach the novel with a detached and dispassionate mind. The paper concludes by saying that Deshpande's novel under consideration is a clarion call for half the world's mute population to break the silence for better family relationship.

The third paper, "'Telling the Other Side of the Story' in Shashi Deshpande's *That Long Silence*", by Veena Dwivedi examines the existential crisis in women's lives and then studies the novel of Deshpande from a gothic point of view. It largely dwells on the strained relationship of Jaya and Mohan in their married life. Because of tension, Jaya becomes only Mohan's wife, and loses her freedom of choice, even her identity and individuality.

The next paper, "Breaking the Barriers: A Study of Shashi Deshpande's *That Long Silence*", by Sanjana Shamshery purports to say that this novel discusses at some length the theme of a married woman struggling against an odd life. Jaya's life becomes miserable when she learns about her husband's malpractices at his office and the impending enquiry against him, setting the prestige of the family at naught. At the close of the paper, Shamshery opines that a meaningful co-existence can be attained in the spousal relationship through mutual understanding and respect, not through domination and subjugation.

Then follows the paper of Sthitaprajna titled "Breaking That Long Silence: The Quest for Space, Identity and Independence". It brings into focus the story of Jaya, the protagonist, and Mohan, her husband, who are ill-matched mentally and temperamentally. Jaya is an educated, middle-class woman, and Mohan is an authoritative and egotistic man. She craves for space, freedom and identity of her own. She is also a sensitive writer. But Mohan does not allow her freedom of writing and imposes restrictions upon her. She feels dwarfed under his tutelage. At last, she develops a philosophic attitude towards life to carry it on with her life-partner.

The sixth paper, "Emancipating the Bonded Self: A Study of Shashi Deshpande's *That Long Silence*", by Monika Mathur studies the intention of Deshpande to break the icy 'silence' of the female protagonist. The silence is partly Jaya's own creation, and partly levied by society and tradition. In a patriarchal society like ours, women are prescribed many 'dos' and 'don'ts' in order to make them merely a child-bearing machine and a follower of male dictates. This clips their wings and ties them to a stake. Their freedom is curtailed and their movement is restricted. Their 'bonded self' longs for fresh air, fresh mind. But the chauvinistic males do not allow them all this. Consequently, they lead a subservient, subordinate life within the four walls of their house. Jaya chooses 'speech' to emancipate herself.

The seventh paper, "Deconstructing, Reconstructing Identities: Shashi Deshpande's *That Long Silence*", by Minakshi Lahkar attempts to show Jaya, first, in her traditional roles as a girl and housewife, and then in her emancipated role. If Jaya has initially accepted the roles of an obedient daughter of Appa and Ai, an affectionate sister of Dinkar (alias Dada), and a loving wife of Mohan, she later on assumes the rational role of responsibility to set her house in order. In other words, she has first to deconstruct her traditional roles/identities and has then to reconstruct her new responsible roles/identities. And this change of roles/identities enables her to overcome the dilemma in her familial relationship. The novel, thus, ends on a note of optimism, as Lahkar puts it.

The eighth and last paper, "Shashi Deshpane's *That Long Silence*: A Critique", by Roopali points out Jaya's unhappy relationship with her husband for seventeen years, resulting in her frustration and failure in life. It calls *That Long Silence* an autobiographical novel, which is written from the feminist perspective.

Besides these papers, offering intelligent critiques of *That Long Silence*, this anthology contains three appendices. They are relevant to understand the vision and art of Shashi Deshpande. Appendix 'A' shows Shashi Deshpande's views on the dilemma of a woman writer. Appendix 'B' deals with the search for self in the shorter fiction (i.e., short stories) of Shashi Deshpande. Now that Deshpande's *Collected Stories* (2003) has been published by Penguin Books India, an independent research-oriented project can be undertaken to highlight this aspect of her art. This appendix as well as the next one—Appendix 'C'—is written by myself. Appendix 'C' traces some dominant recurring metaphors in the novels of Shashi Deshpande. Metaphors are "a sign of genius", as Aristotle says, and they can show the coherence and continuity in the art of a writer.

III

The present collection of critical essays aims to highlight the importance of the text that is explicitly feminist in content and well-structured in form. Its language is lucid and easy to grasp, and its style is unadorned and straightforward. It is a treasure of contemporary Indian English fiction, and as such must be read by fiction-loving people for pleasure and profit.

A.N. Dwivedi

Contributors

Sanjoy Saksena. Professor of English at the University of Allahabad; did his post-doctoral studies in the U.K.; writes papers and articles perceptively.

Ashok Kumar Sharma. Formerly Reader & Head, Department of English, Feroze Gandhi P.G. College, Rai Bareli (U.P.); has written books on Manohar Malgonkar and Manju Kapur; writes good papers and edits *The Expression.*

Veena Dwivedi. Asstt. Professor in English (Humanities) at the Feroze Gandhi College of Engineering and Technology, Rai Bareli; writes research papers intelligently.

Sanjana Shamshery. Associate Professor & Chairperson, Department of English, H.P. University, Shimla (H.P.); guides research scholars and writes papers in reputed journals.

Sthitaprajna. Asstt. Professor in English at IIER, Bhubaneshwar (Odisha); writes perceptive research papers and reviews.

Monika Mathur. Asstt. Professor of English at Maharaja Lakshman Sen Memorial College, Sundar Nagar, Mandi (H.P.); has published articles in reputed national and international journals.

Minakshi Lahkar. Associate Professor of English at Ramanujan College, University of Delhi; an intelligent reviewer and critic.

Roopali. Assistant Professor of English at the Amity University, Lucknow; did her D. Phil. from the University of Allahabad; writes research papers perceptively.

Shashi Deshpande. Celebrated Indian English novelist and short-story writer; lives in Bangalore along with her family; winner of the Sahitya Akademi Award for her novel *That Long Silence* in 1989.

A.N. Dwivedi. Formerly Professor of English at the University of Allahabad, Allahabad (U.P.) and Ex-Professor and Chairman, Department of English at the Taiz University, Al-Turba, Republic of Yemen; has written a dozen of books of literary criticism, three books of translation and five books of English poetry; has contributed over a hundred research papers and articles to well-known Indian and foreign journals. His sixth book of English poetry is in the pipeline; edits *The Journal of Contemporary Literature*.

1
CHAPTER

'Writing of Us' in *That Long Silence*

Sanjoy Saksena

The first thing that struck me after reading *That Long Silence* was that silence can be paradoxical and that in the case of women much as it may indicate their helplessness, it also portends guile and even aggressiveness. It is a sign of weakness but often only apparently for they strike back cruelly with a cold cleverness which escapes the unsuspecting males, overconfident as they may be cue to their gender based advantages that tradition endows on them. There can be no doubt about Shashi Deshpande's feminist sympathies and even after display of strength, the protagonist, Jaya, becomes jittery towards the end about her feminist compulsions and tries to fall in line with the regular female behavioural patterns. In these behavioural inconsistencies it is not difficult to locate specimens from average Indian families or ourselves and this makes the novel at once representative. Within the incongruities and foibles of the characters one can see reflections of several people one tends to come across in the lanes and by-lanes of India, or, in other words, it is all about us. The strength that the woman displays throughout the novel fades away and above all else she gets worried about saving her marriage, even if it meant making compromises with her beliefs. Feminism brought along with it belligerence in India and those women who found it too uncomfortable to openly challenge resorted to devious methods, among their armour tears and silence being all important, for within the traditional set up they worked and in times of crisis gave them the liberty to attack which plain confrontation may have made ungainfully ugly and a losing proposition. Jaya is a silent operator who recognizes silence, reads it well, and uses it to her advantage, cleverly manipulates situations. Silence in *That Long Silence* mostly is a sign of women's vulnerability as well as their subtle behaviour in keeping with domestic politics, often directed against the males in their own interest. The potency of silence is best proved by its success in adverse situations.

When words become redundant, silence is a wiser option and the males of the family too resort to it. The opening sentence of the novel itself gives us a clue as to what the protagonist has up her sleeve to attain independence in her life, marital and joint familial: 'hard and ruthless' behaviour. She also makes it clear at the outset that:

> I'm writing of us. Of Mohan and me. And I know this—you can never be the heroine of your own story. Self-revelation is a cruel process. The real picture, the real 'you' never emerges. Looking for it is as bewildering as trying to know how you really look. Ten different mirrors show you ten different faces. (Deshpande 1)

The mirrors could stand for perspectives and the faces for angles. When viewed from one angle, the face and personality may appear something and from another as something else. It is this something else, the elusive self, that eludes the author-narrator and remains buried in words—appears to be asking as it were to be excavated in the Foucauldian sense.

That Long Silence was published in 1988 by Shashi Deshpande and in the 1990s there developed differences between second and third wave feminists. If we go by what Jennifer Purvis has to tell us, conflict arose over 'heteronormative principles' and 'paradigmatic attachments' which were linked up with generational thought that ended up generating 'unproductive anxieties' (Purvis 93). In the novel Jaya's arrogance is generational, while the more mature and older women try to take on patriarchy from below, after almost acquiescence. This acquiescence itself turned into resistance without creating unnecessary familial discord for they hit back with silence to make their point potently. They made silence speak louder than words to their and women's advantage in general.

Appearances have always been deceptive and it is this deception, whether unconscious self-deception or the inability to understand one's own self and the others, that makes life complex and informs the relationship between Jaya and Mohan Kulkarni. They are husband and wife, yet there is a conflict raging between the two of them because Jaya cannot accept her subordinate position as the second fiddle that traditional Indian values had forced on her. Mohan enjoys an upper hand because when he got married to Jaya, her father was dead, and her poor family had become poorer, was unable to pay any dowry in keeping with the regular practices of the area. He came from a lower middle-class family but was trained to be an engineer, destined to earn well by the laws of probability. When the relationship begins, resentment starts brewing in Jaya's head and heart because she wanted to be her husband's equal partner in the marital game and subsequently tries to dominate her spouse as perhaps most feminists would dream of doing. The matter does not stop here, Mohan's professional success and impressive earnings encourage Jaya to attempt enjoying one-up manship or, if you like, one-up-womanship over her other family members. Feminism was a conscious commitment of Shashi Deshpande as it is in the case of the protagonist, but belief in feminism does not preclude rivalries among women nor does it exclude possibilities of women trying to boss over their weaker and more vulnerable counterparts. All that Jaya wanted in life was to be herself without in the least allowing her family, tradition or husband coming in her way and such possibilities always bothered her.

> Life would go on for us as before, punctuated by dreary quarrels, the children's successes and failures, from each other, from us, our resentment and bitterness, old age for us, perhaps widowhood for me—this was our future. Nothing else was possible for people like us. (Deshpande 4-5)

It is this predictable trajectory that the lives of most women took which haunted Jaya and, having a mind of her own, she tried to make attempts to break the mould. Jaya does write a column and publishes stories, is known in the society which she and her husband move in as an individual. Mohan takes pride in her achievements but often disagrees with her, specially her views as expressed in the media, and speaks about her writings with a pinch of salt because her earnings were paltry.

It is the supposedly broken mould destroyed by Jaya self-consciously that revives itself once she fears that her marriage may come to an end or something untoward may happen to Mohan. She realizes how crucial her husband was for her and the two children—that their well-being and future depended on him because the harsh realities were economic in nature followed by the question of social prestige. Social position for Jaya depended on Mohan's position whose loss could have reduced them to social outcasts. Jaya came from an economically weaker section of the society and the father's death took place when she was just fifteen. She knew the risks that too much adventurism and feminism entailed but she never the less had her share of a lurid affair with Kamat. Kamat was the only one who truly encouraged her driven by love and lust, both, but it was Mohan who was like a 'sheltering tree', as Vanitamami would put it.

Tradition is sought to be questioned but little thought is spared to find out as to how it takes its form and solidifies into a shared belief. It must be distinguished from superstition. Tradition is deterministic in nature and it evolves over years and becomes hard boiled after decades of experiences of all shades of people. The essence is passed from generation to generation and to question it is considered improper because to learn by making mistakes involves paying a rather heavy price which may cost a lot not just to the learner but to other near and dear ones. Traditional advices are not always moralistic as they are commonly understood to be but practical in nature and women have their share of such traditional beliefs which are kept away from the men folk. Vanitamami used the metaphor of the sheltering tree for the husband and her other pieces of advice return to Jaya later buried as they were in her unconscious.

> After so many years, the words came back to me. A sheltering tree. Without the tree, you're dangerously unprotected and vulnerable. This followed logically. And so you have to keep the tree alive and flourishing, even if you have to water it

> with deceit and lies. This too followed, equally logically. But in Saptagiri we had a creeper that was watered and manured assiduously; yet it died—of too much water, of white ants in the manure that destroyed its roots. And so...? (Deshpande 32)

Bits and pieces of advice keep on haunting Jaya. It is the danger of the husband's death and being exposed to the ravages of time, greed and all sorts of cheating and deception that run through Jaya's mind. The ironical blow comes when Vanitamami says that if need be a good wife ought to tell lies and resort to cheating in the interest of the husband because in his welfare and prosperity lay the happiness of the wife. Here, Jaya had been carrying on an affair clandestinely with Kamat and had been even toying with the idea of getting married to him. There are eerie warnings of untimely death, even after all the care and attention had been lavished on the man and the possibilities of a terrible aftermath for women always remained. Vanitamami's advice contained the bitter truths of life that applied to the lives of women. Feminism with its bravado or courage to fight well to overcome the vicissitudes of life moved about in Jaya's mind. On the rebound comes the example of a creeper being destroyed by excessive watering and white ants; the implication being that too much care could be bad for the husband or even lead to his death. What could a more damaging and headstrong reply to a traditional advice which sounds fairly mundane? India, or, more specifically Karnataka and Maharashtra, were backward places where the laws of Manu and third worldish existence applied. Jaya was familiar with the violence that went on in the households of the poor in Saptagiri and Ambegaon. Was Vanitamami not being a feminist of sorts when she was advocating unstinted support for the husband? Can a woman's interests not lie with her husband's interests, especially in the sort of situation in which the family functioned with all sorts of disparities and handicaps? Must a woman always emotionally, economically, and professionally lock horns with her husband? Can the two not be complementary to each other? The possibilities of having multiple identities are not even consciously explored by Jaya who appears to be a greenhorn herself in the gender game.

When we look at *That Long Silence* with Simone de Beauvoir's *The Second Sex* in mind, Jaya's actions appear to be attempts to maintain her identity in a patriarchal world and to maintain her 'sense of the self'. Her defiance of her family and husband, her writing of short stories and columns clearly indicate that by doing so she was trying to reclaim her subjectivity. If Jaya was selfishly independent it was because she was attempting 'a cultivation of the self'. All her actions and thoughts indicate "what it might mean to be independent, intellectual and female" (Curthoys 4). Quarrels over small things and men making unreasonable demands on their wives were common. Jaya derives 'strength' from her feminist ideology but alongside it "a despair so great that it would not voice itself. I saw a struggle so bitter that silence was the only weapon. Silence and surrender" (Deshpande 36). Such were the bleak realities of lower middle-class life and they could not be changed easily for the first requirement was wiping off poverty and then a change of mind. Women of the family died in suffering and were remembered little and talked of even less. Childless Vimala suffers from an ovarian tumour and is ridiculed to such an extent that she dies within seven days, without quite being able to explain how she felt about her condition—emotional, physical and financial. Death is a release but nobody cares for her memory. Surrounded by such sorrows Jaya realizes how important it was to possess worldly success and it was in the middle of this grind of poverty that she wanted to make a mark in the world: the obsessive beauty of feminism and her quest to become a person in her own right. Her quest is not entirely triumphal but the attempt makes the woman a cut above the rest, a pale faced model of nerves and some talent. When other women had given up in the family, Jaya continues to struggle because within her small family circle, husband and children, she was secure, certainly not under any real threat. The threat was primarily a self-perception and a delusion that came from within due to her flirting with feminist ideas. Jaya's brand of feminism at one level becomes highly complex and unleashes contested meanings of feminism, her sudden relapse and surrender does not rule out the possibilities of it surfacing again with greater vitality. A sympathetic critic would call it nuanced feminism that could save her the trouble of seeing her family crumble and split.

Jaya was an educated girl who understood feminist thought and she confesses to it throughout the novel. There is nothing militant about her feminism for it remains a desire to seek self-gratification and she was not prepared deep down to divorce Mohan or simply give him up due to his suspected liaison with some other woman. Kamat was her admirer and facilitator but no substitute for the more successful Mohan. The crisis that befalls Jaya and Mohan's poor relatives reinforces the woman's desire for greater autonomy, wealth and security. The couple remember their lower middle-class background and aspire for more money, even if it meant making compromises with integrity. Feminism does not prevent Jaya from trying to get more comforts and wealth for herself and she continues to look down upon the more helpless women in the family nor does she bother to check out on Mohan's underhand dealings. Her concern for the poor cousins and aunts is superficial and not genuine. Jaya is only too happy to inherit the flat which her Dada wanted to gift her in Bombay despite the bypassed Vanitamami's repeated protests. Vanitamami had a right to her husband's property and feminism does not prevent Jaya to kick her aside: self-interest governs her actions and they show the hollowness inside her brand of feminism in which the self and personal interests are paramount. She remains least bothered about the resentment shown by Geeta, Dada's wife. While she brushes aside Vanitamami's assertion of her right to property, she revels in the past activities of the old woman's husband, Makarandmama, who was associated with the Bombay talkies and Devika Rani, the star actress of yesteryears.

She takes vicarious pleasure in the memory of the forbidden pleasures that Makarandmama enjoyed as a marginal actor but does not relent when confronted with Vanitamami's pleadings with 'dogged tenacity' or the old woman's declaration that it was to her that Makarand had gifted the flat before going to the sanatorium at Panchgani. In family politics Jaya pokes fun at Kusum and Vanitamami, the two weak females, who had managed to survive and for them in Jaya's heart there is scorn and recognition of their survival instincts—'terrible tenacity of the weak'. It is Mohan who removes the photographs of Makarandmama from the house without qualms. On the one hand, Jaya and Mohan were enjoying luck with property and professional success, but on the other their son had moved away from books and the daughter, Rati, found pleasure in comic books not textbooks. Mohan's intimidating patriarchal presence scares the children to go to their school books but not enough to make them concentrate on their studies. Jaya does not mind this patriarchal intimidation at all, no resentment trespasses her imagination, on the contrary she hopes that it would be in the children's interests. Children are given heavy doses of morality, commitment to work and the necessity of success; but the couple combine together to maintain secrecy about the enquiry that had been ordered against Mohan for corruption. The double-faced contradictions in the conduct of Mohan and Jaya become obvious and their vulgar desire to succeed in life through foul means.

If Mohan had his share of corruption charges, Jaya had her sultry affair with Kamat; children were not supposed to know too much about their parents. While all this was going on, the duo does not fail to pity the maid-servant, Jeeja, who was regular with and devoted to her work and whose 'sole purpose in life was to go living'. Her silent and stoic acceptance of her fat and jobless husband arouses pity and amusement; never compels Jaya to take a peep within herself—look at the self-obsessed feminism that she had callously kept alive in her heart. Jaya, in the scheme of things, always puts herself above all else and is, unlike Jeeja, free from all the elements of sacrifice. Jeeja was a dedicated worker and a straight woman, unlike the couple who would stoop to succeed, butter their bread. Corruption is casually accepted by Jaya and Mohan, it is only the issues involved in being found out that bother them. The contrast between a rich and a subaltern woman is sharp and it indicates how the upper crust of the Indian society functions in a slick manner, feminism and Gandhianism are no hindrances. It is because of this duplicity that the Indian brand of feminism and feminists have come under heavy fire from those who do not subscribe to their beliefs. Jaya cosily narrates the helplessness of Jeeja and her husband who had suffered because of a strike at the factory and with a Janus face discusses the plight of Tara's family and then she moves on to contemplate the inhuman treatment of girls in the past century with a false sense of injury.

> Where was it I had read an account of how baby girls were done to death a century or so back? They were, I had read in horror, buried alive, crushed to death in the room they were born in; and immediately after that, a fire was lit on the spot—to purify the place, they said. Perhaps it was to ensure death. (Deshpande 53)

It is precisely this kind of concern that does not go down well with the people for the double standards make all observations appear shallow and fake. It serves as a warning to all feminists to be careful in their activism because otherwise the people would reject them and their agenda. What Mrs. Jaya Kulkarni fails to highlight is the collusion of women in such ghoulish practices and her own doubts whether this was better than allowing them to suffer the worst kind of indignities and miseries in later life, show how a devilish practice could be understood as a lesser evil with convenience—weaken the shock of its horrendous nature and dilute the process of reform. Visible in the novel are double-standards galore! Jaya continues to remain dismissive towards ordinary women in her family because they do not realize the seriousness of the issues that feminism proposes to take up and she remains equally dismissive towards those who are antifeminists or 'have adopted' no, but..."version of feminism" (Hall & Rodriguez 878). Many of those who have written off feminism are those who never were a part of it, never did bother to understand it and are pleased to be against it as much due to patriarchal domination as to their 'fear of feminism' and its risks. But a backlash against feminism is clearly visible, yet some of them have decided to push ahead as Jaya does in the novel.

Shashi Deshpande by exposing the paradoxes that run through Indian feminism is trying to strengthen it and it is only when we see the seamy side of the picture that we often struggle to make amends, ameliorate our lot and discover our solutions.

On the one hand, sympathy, indignation and anger of women for improvement of women's lot, and on the other collusion in matters relating to dishonest practices was bound to obfuscate the real women's issues. If the novel has any reformist intentions they are bound to be defeated by such revelations. It is the tragedy of the double standards of the educated and the well-informed that renders them impotent and words and thoughts lose all power. It is this tragic fate of feminists that has made reform too slow a process in India, even invited a strapping reaction. Jaya's empty kindness for Jeeja and Tara and later for Manda and the desire to push herself as a writer ahead with lusty Kamat's help and the tendency to partake in the pleasures and joys that Mohan's ill begotten wealth brought proves that her brand of feminism was too opportunistic, self-centred and mean. She does not even spare her close relatives, intoxicated by the bribes that Mohan brought home. Kusum is an object of pity and a regular joke. Jaya cleverly tries to be evasive when it comes to rescuing them from financial distress even though she had experienced poverty till the day she had got married. Mohan also remains indifferent towards her relatives and is preoccupied mostly with the idea of getting richer unscrupulously. When political trouble breaks out in Bombay which had a completely different temper from Saptagiri, Jaya is overwhelmed by the huge turn out of people in support of Shiv Sena rallies and she watches the 'uniform ugliness' and mobs. There is hardly any political or social empathy in Jaya and the anger of the marching people makes her worried about her own self.

> I felt threatened, and not by the men, nor by the violence I could feel simmering in them. I had a queer sensation, as if something was breaking up, a design or a pattern I was familiar with. Without it, I would have to face the unknown.... (Deshpande 54)

The desperate condition of the country, the impending socio-political disaster, do not make her worry about the state or society: it is the self, the impact that it would have on her own future that appeared more uncertain in the changing milieu and ethos. The Shiv Sena, being an extreme right wing Hindu political outfit, sought, among other things, revival of the traditional Hindu way of life in which the women were bound to suffer. In the name of Hindu tradition they would be pushed back and the feminist ambitions would take a beating.

Later, as time passes away Jaya and Mohan become silent and are scared of the silence of the masses that they perceive as also by the silence that attends the couple next door. The quarrel that breaks out and explodes among the couple next door is over the charge of a lack of fidelity in the woman and this rings a bell about the silent nature of the relationship between Jaya and Mohan, the possibilities of there being an explosion of sorts between them, which does not happen, can also be connected with the likelihood of violence in Bombay and the nation where many grave issues had combined to ferment widespread trouble. The moment Mohan is at peace with himself he starts enjoying his promotion and calls all those looking for a social change 'irresponsible callous men' because he was prospering in the corrupt system that they wished to get rid of. Jaya compares herself with Gandhari, one of the characters in the *Mahabharat*, and like she comfortably ignored husband Dhritrashtra's indiscretions, is happy to ignore the sly practices that Mohan was adopting to move ahead in his career. To justify her acceptance of Mohan's wrongs and her own dubious collusion in his activities she calls Gandhari 'an ideal wife'.

Shashi Deshpande loses no opportunity in the novel to paint the pathetic lot of women and in order to do so she introduces several sub-plots into the main structure of the novel cleverly. We are reminded that rigorous codes of conduct, expectations of traditional patriarchy and the sheer force of habit formed due to living under crushing domination for centuries reduced most women to the level of dim wits. Deshpande employs black humour to drive her point home and it does shake us up for among the victims could be members from our own families and even among our friend circle. Women generally fast for their husbands because it is on them that their welfare after marriage depends and most women, unlike Jaya, did not work for a living or were capable of making a living independently. Both Mukta and Vanitamami appear to be caricaturish figures because they practised whatever was supposed to be their *dharma,* even though it was not practically required.

> If it wasn't her 'Saturday', it was 'her Monday', or 'her Thursday'. Mukta had more days of fasts than days on which she ate a normal meal. Her self-mortification seemed to be the most positive thing about her. And yet her piety—surely it was that which prompted those fasts?—seemed meaningless, since she had already forfeited the purpose of it, the purpose of all Hindu women's fasts—the avoidance of widowhood.
>
> Mukta's fasts reminded me of Vanitamami's *pujas* and fasts. Perhaps Vanitamami had begun the discipline when there had still been the hope in her of having children; but she had gone on with her fasts, her ritual circumambulations of the *tulsi* plant, of the *peepul* tree, even when their aim had gone beyond her reach, when her uterus had shrivelled and her ovaries atrophied. Maybe it had become a habit by then, a habit she could not forsake. (Deshpande 67)

The fear of becoming a widow and not having children was endemic to women and the thought about Ai as a widow sobers down Jaya because her mother was too close to her and also because she could not be clinically satirical about her. No woman, not in the twenty-first century, at least, would approve of such acts of devotion and belief in the divine intervention.

The second wave feminism after the Second World War gave birth to concern for the quality of life among women of the western world. This was the result of their having attained reasonably high material levels of existence, but in India it was so because under their impact Indian women too started searching for a better life as does Jaya Kulkarni. She does not hesitate to ruminate on matters relating to sex and abortion, and tries to support the equal opportunities agenda, matters that were considered a taboo. It is as a consequence of the 'equality revolution' that she competes with her husband to make a mark in the outside world and within her family, tries to force a value change among her relatives where women were too old fashioned in their beliefs. In India the society remained poor, but Mohan and Jaya became a part of the creamy upper crust and therefore for Jaya 'affection, self-esteem, and self-expression' became more important (Hayes et al. 425-29). Once Jaya gets married she gradually enters a post-materialistic value-system and non-materialistic matters become greater compulsions despite her childhood brushes with debilitating poverty. However, the past is never eradicated or obliterated from her memory, conflicting attitudes surface in times of crisis.

Jaya always felt threatened in her husband's presence, felt that she was the second fiddle and that their relationship was following the acceptable model of the male dominating with ease. However, when she has a tiff with Mohan over her cooking and silence follows for days it was Mohan who was the worse affected and he succumbs, starts talking to her first.

It is then that Jaya realizes her 'awesome power over him'. But this does not mean that the relationship had become completely stable and one-sided for it continued to be complex in which love was not a simple, uncomplicated affair. Jaya starts perceiving Mohan as an 'adversary more hostile' than she had 'imagined'. He would try to dominate with the use of anger and Jaya being a woman was forced to cringe. She tries to come close to Ravi but it does not work out and the relationship takes an unpredictable path to a damp ending.

> Each relationship evolves its own vocabulary. Ours had been that of the workaday world. The vocabulary of love, which I had thought would come naturally and inevitably, had passed us by; so too had the vocabulary of anger. No, it was I who had left that alone after the day when my first disastrous foray into verbalising emotions had almost ripped our marriage apart. Since then, we'd never gone beyond those first basic *mudras*. Now suddenly, unfairly, he'd overtaken me. His fingers flickered, creating images, not of beauty, but of darkness and deceit. (Deshpande 116)

Tension within the marriage had grown and partly responsible for it was Mohan's professional ambitions and entanglements with corruption which laced with politics that went on within the couple's extended family made matters miserable. When Jaya tries to express her love for him to ease the growing discord, Mohan's reaction was so hostile that it almost threatened to break their marital bonds.

In his touch, especially finger movements on her body, she perceives an unknown threat in which cheating seemed to be present. The guilt inside Jaya recoils in the form of perverse sexual experiences which gave her no pleasure but only more thoughts and apprehensions to worry about. Mohan's mind after his close parleys with Agarwal, his colleague, had started wandering in the direction of manipulation and strategic maneuvering to save himself and Jaya, his co-sharer of ill-begotten money, who he felt was indifferent towards his difficulties. Her taking refuge in tears wasn't enough to satisfy him nor was sexual gratification any kind of permanent relief. The relationship takes a beating and Jaya's confession about never truly being in love with him exposes the hollowness that defined their arranged marriage.

> Somewhere a radio was blaring out a film song...'Come back, my love, come back to me'. But Mohan was not my love, he had never been that; he told me, 'You've never cared for me.' Then what have I been doing, living with him all these years? (Deshpande 124)

Indifference described the relationship best and both Jaya and Mohan were aware of their loss of interest in each other, it were the children and the need to be somebody's spouse in society that kept them together. If the children kept the woman's mind away from such botherations, the memory of unhinged Kusum made her feel as though she belonged to "the category of unwanted wives, deserted wives". Solace comes in the form of traditional Hindu thought which says that "marriages never end, they cannot—they are a state of being" (Deshpande 127). Thus, after mulling over such lofty thoughts her mind goes back to the abortion she had undergone without even informing Mohan and never did let him know all that she had done secretly. Her mind even explores the possibility of becoming a widow and amusingly this possibility provides her some mental comfort because a widow does not have a husband to hassle her. She completely forgets what her Ai had to undergo as a widow. Jaya's woes get compounded when Ramu Kaka tells her that after marriage she did not belong to the family she was born in—that she belonged to Mohan's family—that she had 'no place' in her own father's house out of the family tree that she was.

Angela McRobbie has argued that those who denied the label of feminism and preferred to remain free floating ideologically have been pushed into the background, both socially and politically. Within the family too due to the more dynamic younger set they have been relegated into the background. McRobbie's contention is that feminism is also responsible for the stratification among women in society and it manifests itself in economic disparity wherein elitist women like Jaya have comfortably given a short shrift to those who do not think alike. The 'Third Way' which addresses the problems of women outside the movement and supports a more egalitarian and balanced approach politically and socially is precisely that which Shashi Deshpande's protagonist sweeps aside without any compunctions and tries to seduce women into the feminist ideological beliefs stealthily. Therefore, *That Long Silence* instead of being all inclusive encourages a divisiveness among women themselves. Kusum and Vanitamami become the butt of many a joke at their expense and Ai etc. remain marginal characters. The Third Way encourages a women's movement which would be all inclusive in which feminism would not be a driving force at all, especially after postfeminism became more popular. "This is partly because feminism now occupies the peculiar position of being seemingly universally disliked, while at the same time it has crept into the realm of popular common sense" (McRobbie 99).

When Jaya goes on introspecting deeper into her relationship with Mohan, she discovers that he was not in the least concerned whether she was writing good or bad short stories. He is dismissive towards the short story in which she wrote about a man who could only become close to his wife, 'through her body'. Such stuff was dismissed as exhibitionism by her husband when she was looking for praise. It was this dismissiveness that hurts her and makes her suffer from a sense of self-reproach because the anger that broke out often was 'jeopardizing the only career I had, my marriage'. Retrospection in Jaya makes her feel miserable because she had behaved like a 'Smart Alec' with Kusum and Vanitamami. She is convinced that she had, "Irrelevant, middle-class, bourgeoise" propensities because she talks about the shame that had been heaped on women for decades, including shaving of the head of widows and being called whores. She displays international sympathies with women who were raped in Bangla Desh and Vietnam, is concerned about the fate of people living in these countries as well as of the Jews as recorded by Annie Frank. Beneath all this was her compromise with Mohan's corruption and making fun of Kusum and Vanitamami, her giving top priority to make her marriage work even if it meant humiliating adjustments. The duplicity makes a sham out of her feminism and her idealism appears phony.

Jaya's interest in Kamat does not flail because he tries to encourage her to write with passion and attempts to convince her that she needed to make her writings more bold and vigorous because he perceives that her feminist concerns demanded strength rather than restraint. Kamat's gut feeling was that she was holding her anger back which could have informed her writings: "spew out your anger in your writing, woman, spew it out" (Deshpande 147). It does occur to Kamat that Jaya's writings were perhaps as limp as they were because her feminism was not genuine; it had an undercurrent of selfishness which made it inadequate, irresolute and ineffectual. The conversation between him and Jaya becomes a heated one and goes on predictably feminist lines, becomes Shashi Deshpande's invitation to her readers to think more intensely about the plight of educated women who wish to pursue a career and make their marriages thrive. The point is that women's anger, their outbursts and logic does not go down well with the men, even those who are sympathetic in the Indian sense. One almost imagines that Shashi Deshpande has shoved bits and pieces of a feminist harangue into the unwilling mouths of some of her characters in order to provoke us to think, shake us out of complacency. One of the problems that arose out of feminism pertained to sexual autonomy and freedom. This became a sore point for those who do not encourage sexual promiscuity, even if it be for the sake of feminist ideology, authentic self-hood, and intellectual independence as was the case with Jaya. A backlash was bound to be there from the family and society if she had been discovered in a compromising position with Kamat.

Pat Horn has argued that feminism is in a state of disarray because of its various shades of political and ideological leanings which generate conflict and divisions among women themselves (Horn 71). She has based her arguments on the basis of her experiences in South Africa which is a third world country not very different, gender-wise, from India. Pat Horn has tried to plead in support of a reworking of strategies and visions, something which Deshpande's novel assists in by highlighting the complexities and contradictions in women's lives. Jaya attacks the male's inability to understand women and the unprofitable things that women must do to make their married lives happy, whatever happiness may mean. Kamat on the other hand alleges that such stuff was "a soft, squishy bog of self-pity" that would interfere with the quality of her writing and all that she desired to achieve for herself through it. He discovers a martyr syndrome at work inside the woman and a tendency to mimic the feminists that lowered the quality of her creative work. Perhaps, these are problems that beset Shashi Deshpande's fiction itself and in this sense the novel becomes autobiographical. The harshness of the reality and of success within the prevailing brutal reality made Jaya look for a feminist cubby hole to be comfortable in because matters were becoming unbearable for her. She did not like the idea of becoming vulnerable as a family woman and as an aspiring writer. 'Seeta' gave Jaya satisfaction but it also often invited adverse comments that shook her out of her snug existence which the cleverly begotten wealth had endowed on her. Possibilities of failure as a writer are too upsetting and no less disturbing are the thoughts of failing as a wife and mother. This is why she says that it was only possible to enjoy a 'perfect relationship' with the dead. As for the living men and women, relationships between them were anything but natural: "only treachery, only deceit, only betrayal". She confesses openly in the novel—"guile had been my weapon".

When Mukta enquires about the trouble that had been brewing between Jaya and Mohan Kulkarni, she realizes that guile does not always succeed, even when the most clever handle it. Mohan leaves the home and goes away without informing Jaya. Jaya is all shaken up and her imagination is aflame with all kinds of perverse possibilities. She surmises whether it was because of Kamat or some other woman or accident that he had disappeared into the thin air. The militant feminism that had surfaced in front of Kamat disappears before Mukta. Searching questions haunt her:

> I'll tell you what's wrong. I've failed him. He expected something from me, from his wife, and I've failed him. All these years I thought I was Mohan's wife; now he tells me I was never that, not really. What am I going to do? What shall I do if he doesn't come back? Mukta, I was so confident, so sure of myself, I felt so superior to others...Kusum, yes, and you too...and now, without Mohan, I'm...I don't know, I don't know what I am. (Deshpande 185)

Gnawing fears about an impending marital disaster loom large and Jaya realizes by looking deep into the innermost recesses of her heart that her marriage was on the rocks due to her faults. She feels that if she loses Mohan she may be finished for it was her husband who provided her all the security and Kamat, the second option, was dead. The airs that she had assumed within the family and inside the society had vanished within minutes.

She feels that her identity itself may be finished and all that she had been imagining herself to be was dependent on that one single man. Her pride in herself evaporates. While she recognizes this, she does not fail to admit that hers had been a loveless marriage: "we lived together but there had been only emptiness between us" (Deshpande 185). It is Mukta who blames Jaya for making her marriage empty because of her entanglement with Kamat and to counter her allegation Jaya keeps repeating that she was Mohan's wife to contradict the sad fact that she had drifted away from her spouse in search of love, emotional fulfilment and encouragement elsewhere. Towards the end of the novel, she admits that she had cut off those "bits that refused to be Mohan's wife" (Deshpande 191). Jaya in the end emerges as a fence sitter feminist like many of them in India have been always and "in the embracing of ambiguity, they truly remained on the fence" (Aronson 916). There was nothing definite about the protagonist's brand of feminism and it were the arising situations that let it evolve in keeping with the demands of the prevailing time. After the heavy jolt that Mohan gives Jaya, discretion emerges as the better part of valour and the subsequent actions of the woman point towards peaceful directions. Shashi Deshpande brings in Daniel Defoe's concept of fiction as something in between facts and lies. Lies may well be the imagination at work—a world that we create within ourselves; inscapes. Our psychology is such that we cannot experience objective reality which becomes subjective in our minds and hearts—some being more prone to such phenomena than others. When Mohan's telegram arrives, proclaiming as it were, that all was well, Jaya feels that silence between husband and wife could be dreadful and that there was a need for them to open up. The novel is open-ended and to make it thus Shashi Deshpande again relies on Jaya's imagination which works overtime as they say and she thinks that there could be an element of shock present in the surprise.

BIBLIOGRAPHY

Aronson, Pamela. "Feminists or 'Postfeminists': Younger Women's Attitudes towards Feminism and Gender Relations." *Gender and Society,* Vol. 17, No. 6, Dec. 2003.

Curthoys, Ann. "Adventures of Feminism: Simone de Beauvoir's Autobiographies, Women's Liberation, and Self-Fashioning." *Feminist Review,* No. 64, Spring 2000.

Deshpande, Shashi. *That Long Silence.* New Delhi: Penguin Books, 1989.

Hall, Eliane J. and Marnie Salupo Roderiguez. "The Myth of Postfeminism." *Gender and Society,* Vol. 17, No. 6, December 2003.

Hays, Bernadette C., Ian McAllister and Donley T. Studlar. "Gender, Postmaterialism, and Feminism in Comparative Perspective."

International Political Science Review/Revue internationale de science politique, Vol. 21, No. 4, October 2000.

Horn, Pat. "Where is Feminism Now?" *Agenda,* No. 6, 1995.

McRobbie, Angela. "Feminism and the Third Way." *Feminist Review,* No. 64, Spring 2000.

Purvis, Jennifer. "Girls and Women Together in the Third Wave: Embracing the Challenges of Intergenerational Feminism(s)." *NWSA Journal,* Vol. 16, No. 3, Autumn 2004.

2

CHAPTER

Defamiliarization of Self-Script in Shashi Deshpande's *That Long Silence*

Ashok Kumar Sharma

There are several novels which have been labeled as autobiographical novels. The most known and loved novels in this category are *The Vicar of Wakefield, Pride and Prejudice, David Copperfield, Sons and Lovers* and *A Farewell to Arms*. These are all timeless creations of art. Moreover, autobiography and novel are the two distinct genres. It will debase the one if one genre leaks into the other. Shashi Deshpande's *That Long Silence* may be a chit of her past life but not her autobiography in any way and in any sense. The often used phrase, the autobiographical novel, is a very ambiguous term and it does not fit to many celebrated novels, though they give the illusion of autobiography. Rushdie's *Midnight's Children* and Shashi Deshpande's *That Long Silence* are such novels, which defy the above term. Self-reflections may appear in certain episodes and through certain characters which by and large identify with the real characters. But to connect these items with the life story of the creator will be incorrect.

One must understand that the novel is a literary genre and a modern epic in contemporary times. A tool which reflects social, political and historical facts of the world in which we live. But one must remember that the literary world and the real world are different in sense and sensibility. They give reader an illusion of reality. Actually this illusion is the outcome of the novelist's craftsmanship. Here, we can equate the word craftsmanship with technique. Before analyzing the novel *That Long Silence* and the protagonists Jaya and Mohan, we shall discuss the psychology of the readers with regard to such novels.

It is the human psychology that we try to connect the known with the unknown and the unknown with the known. It is very easy to find out clues in order to connect with the known facts related to the author's life. Readers with one or two evidences declare the whole text as the self-script of the novelist. Sometimes authors too in interviews disclose to have used some very personal experiences in their work. Publishers too highlight such items for commercial gains. But in truth autobiography cannot be a novel and *vice versa*. And both need a different treatment.

It is through the following two examples we would try to remove the misconception of labelling a said novel as autobiographical. D.H. Lawrence's *Sons and Lovers* (1913) is the first such example. It is said that it is the story of Lawrence and Jessie Chambers who could not cement their relationship in an everlasting bond due to his mother Lydia Lawrence's interference. But the novel has several deviations from the actual story of the author's life. D.H. Lawrence in *Sons and Lovers* kills his father in the novel. Critics have said that Lawrence has shown his father in a bad light. Jessie Chambers in her memoirs criticizes D.H. Lawrence for misrepresenting her in his novel. She in her memoirs has called Lawrence a puritan, afraid of sex, disturbed by the difference he felt existing between physical and spiritual love, and so on. According to Graham Hough, *Sons and Lovers* is a wishful fictionalizing of an unpleasant truth.

As the second example, we take up Ernest Hemingway's *A Farewell to Arms* (1929), which depicts his experience of the First World War in Italy where he was wounded by a mortar and was nursed in a base hospital in Milan. It is said that there he fell in love with an American nurse of Polish ancestry, namely Agnes Von Kurowsky, but he failed to win her as his wife. In the novel Frederic Henry and Catherine Barkley are the hero and the heroine and there are several deviations from the actual life story of the author.

One must understand from the above two examples that a novel might be based on the personal experiences of the writer, but all the same it is a novel, not a direct and exact transcript of life. And what an eminent writer tries to do is not to provide a catalogue of his own observations and felt experiences but to communicate an integrated and ordered vision of life. With this aim, he reshapes and reorganizes the total experiences in response to artistic exigencies.

Shashi Deshpande's *That Long Silence* (1988) is a great novel if we evaluate it as a novel and separate it from its subjective element. The novel centres around Jaya the heroine who is the pivot around whom the total action of the novel revolves. The title of the novel serves as a metaphor for the suppressed Indian woman. Rashmi Gaur in one of her articles, entitled "Images of Indian Woman in Shashi Deshpande's *That Long Silence*" avers:

> Her work passionately concentrates on the predicament of women and men are pushed toward the periphery; her plots and subplots provide a pointer to the catatonic status of women in the tradition bound, male dominated middle class society of contemporary India in which they are struggling to overcome the constructing dilemmas of prefixed definitions and present norms and thus attempting to redefine their status. (Rashmi, *Pegasus* 33)

Shashi Deshpande's fifth novel, *That Long Silence,* really tries to break the ice and exhorts the Indian women for emancipation. That long silence is broken by words, deeds and silent revolution of a set of women characters. Deshpande's quotation from Elizabeth Robins is meaningful as it carries the theme of Deshpande's novel. "If I were a man and cared to know the world I lived in, I almost think it would make me a shade uneasy—the weight of that long silence of one half of the world" (*That Long Silence*).

Let us see how in the novel Indian women of the middle class in tradition-bound male-dominated society behave and also what treatment they get from their male counterparts. It is not the story of a particular family, it may be a story of any family—Punjabi, Bengali, Tamil or any of the families of Indian peninsula. Moreover, it is not the first time that an educated Indian woman of the middle class is made to suffer and to suffocate and where even to register a protest is regarded as a disobedience. Manju Kapur's six novels, from *Difficult Daughters* to *The Immigrants,* portray the woman's perpetual struggle against the double standard of society. Prior to Manju Kapur, Rama Mehta and Anita Desai in *Inside the Haveli* (1977) and *Fire on the Mountain* (1977) have portrayed it. Shashi Deshpande's novel can only be evaluated in the proper light when we strip it off from its subjective decorative cover. Deshpande can be credited for two things. First, her real life experiences have undergone the process of defamiliarization through her narrative technique which has made her novel look as a universal story of a middle class family—or look as a 'Ghar Ghar Ki Kahani'. Secondly, Deshpande portrays and contrasts the females of three generations. A contrasting study of conscious and unconscious females. Some are conscious of their basic rights and some are not. But first we shall talk of this defamiliarization of known and felt experiences in the process of creative writing.

In the second decade of the last century, Russian formalists brought some changes in an analysis of literary works. They were called formalists and they were against the consideration of politics in literature. Obviously, "Formalism and Marxism were mutually irrelevant because the former explained existence from the inside and the latter from the outside" (John Halperin *Theory of the Novel* 380). Of the very important members of the group such as Boris Tomashersky, Boris Eichenbaum, Roman Jacobson and others, the most important and impressive member of this early group was Victor Shklovsky. Shklovsky has put his views on art in his seminal essay "Art as Technique" (1917). In this essay he has presented his theory of defamiliarization. According to him, a creative artist creates his own fictional world by defamiliarization of his felt experiences. This creates a space for technique and with the help of his technique or literary devices he succeeds in defamiliarizing the familiar and known objects. Regarding this technique of Shklovsky, Halperin says:

> To focus upon specific literary techniques...is to perceive the author's universe by perceiving the author himself at work. Defamiliarization forces the reader to perceive technique by making the familiar seem strange and calling attention to its strangeness through wordplay, syntax, metaphor and other literary devices. (*Theory of the Novel* 380)

It is not the technique but the artfulness of the object that is important. Like Ortega, Shklovsky also believed in the attraction and calling attention of the reader towards the fictional world. John Halperin puts this aspect of the two in the following words:

> The work of art after all need not refer to anything outside itself. Like Ortega, Shklovsky believes that art must attract and hold our attention within its own world. Perception becomes, then, an end in itself; "morality" lies in full awareness, and art is the record of and occasion for that awareness. The effect of the greatest literature is to make man exceptionally aware. Art, however, teaches man less about his world than its own. It is always the world rather than the real one that Formalism emphasizes. (*Theory of the Novel* 380-81)

It is in reference to the theory of Victor Shklovsky that we evaluate Shashi Deshpande's *That Long Silence.* The story of a south-western family with nothing new in the text has been defamiliarized and has been made to look attractive and novel. This she has done with the help of ancient puranic style of narration in which we find a story within a story and it continues till the end. Such narratives are always open-ended. Secondly, the novelist employs different metaphors, symbols and contrasting study of characters and places to make his narrative attractive.

In *That Long Silence*, Deshpande narrates the story of three generations of a middle class family in a very engaging and attractive way. There is a first generation of Azzi, Appa and Aai. Azzi is a widow and the life of a widow in pre-independence India has been presented sympathetically:

> Azzi, a shaven widow had denuded herself of all those things that make-up a woman's life. She had no possession absolutely none apart from the two saries she wore. Her

> room was bare, except for the large bed on which my grandfather had slept, a bed which ever since I knew it was unburdened by a mattress. (*TLS* 28)

Appa, Ramu Kaka, Luxman Kaka, Jaya lived in Saptagiri and Jaya's two brothers, Dinkar and Ravi, also began their life there. Appa told Jaya that her name Jaya stood for victory. When Appa died, Jaya who was very close to her father felt the vacuum. Jaya shows her sense of loss in the following words:

> One morning, soon after Appa's death, I woke up and remembered that he was dead. And I had a sense of loss that was not vague but specific. I thought of that place where he should have at that moment on his bed. And with a picture of his absence from that bed, there was a terrifying sense of emptiness in me. (*TLS* 66)

After her father, it was Dada (elder brother) in whom she reposed her trust. It was on her Dada's persuasion that Jaya married Mohan, an engineer. She had also a great affection for her younger brother, Ravi. The relationship between Jaya and Mohan was laid on the foundation of mutual love, respect and trust. But a sense of male superiority eroded their relationship. In his job Mohan could not sail smoothly and not only at Lohagarh but in Bombay too he found himself in problem. On the other hand, Jaya took to writing and became popular due to her column 'Sita' in a magazine but had to leave her writing to save her relationship with Mohan.

Ambegaon, the place of Jaya's maternal home, has also been graphically drawn. Chandumama and Makarandmama—two diverse maternal uncles—have been portrayed finely. Vanitamami and her niece Kusum have been drawn as weak females. Kusum's tragic death shows the vulnerability of women who are not well supported. However, you can keep both Kusum and Jaya on the same side. But one is negative and the other is positive. And both inescapably suffer. Rashmi Gaur in her research paper brings to light the plight of women:

> *That Long Silence* presents the stereotypes and myths about Indian feminity through various peripheral characters. In the beginning of the novel the character of Kusum is portrayed

> as a counterfoil to Jaya who mirrors the darker regions of her psyche. She is a touchstone against which Jaya tests and ensures her sanity and normalcy. Kusum, carrying "an aura of defeat about her" (23), represents a way of life in which women are made keenly aware of the low position they occupy in their society. (*Pegasus* 35)

Not only Kusum, Vimla, Vanitamami and Mukta are the sufferers, but Jaya is also in the same boat with all the outward glitter, education and well-placed husband. She feels the worthlessness of her life. Rashmi Gaur rightly avers:

> Jaya was aware of an inner void, a hollowness in her life even though it was shielded by the deceptively beautiful screen of her social graces and obligations. (*Pegasus* 35)

Jaya is sincere, responsible, cooperative and educated but still she suffers. Kusum and Jaya are the two sides of the same coin. From the point of view of a feminist, in the 20th century these women are the second sex, and the second citizens of a free country. Shashi Deshpande has successfully portrayed a variety of female species who come from different pockets of the country.

In the novel, Rahul, Rati and Neelima stand for the third generation. Particularly the attitude of Rahul, who runs away from the company of Mohan's family friends, stands for the revolt against the parents. His nature has been contrasted with that of Rati. This also shows that women adapt to new situations early and fast. In the same way, Saptagiri and Ambegaon, the Churchgate flat and the Dadar flat have also been contrasted. Some characters such as Kamat, Dilip and Nayana are amazing as they add spice to the total story of the novel.

Since the family shown in the novel is a traditional middle class family, nothing revolutionary and outrageous has been shown. Some stereotype and traditional concepts as regards to Indian woman have been presented through a couple of metaphors, such as "a pair of bullocks" for husband and wife, "a sheltering tree" for husband. References to Ganapati Pooja, Gauri Mangla Pooja, Karvachauth, and various fasts and rituals have been made.

Another significant feature in her novels has been to show the travails of women writers. In *That Long Silence,* Jaya takes up the pen to work for a column in a magazine but she has to give it up. Rashmi Gaur in "Female Sexuality and Introspection in Shashi Deshpande's *Moving On*" points out,

> The figure of a woman writer, her struggles to publish and be accepted and her concerns about the limitation of her craft, is again a common phenomenon in Deshpande's novels. Jaya in *That Long Silence,* Indu in *Roots and Shadows* and Madhu in *Small Remedies* are some examples. (*IJES,* Vol. 42: 33)

Woman has to suffer and surrender her individuality while working as a writer. Social norms often change in case of women serving as a journalist or a writer and they have to cross hurdles one after another. Perhaps the male-dominated society does not want to give her space. Jaya has become a metaphor for all such women writers in *That Long Silence.*

In the beginning, we have contested the terming of the novel *That Long Silence* as an autobiographical novel. Now while concluding the paper once again, we emphasize that Shashi Deshpande in *That Long Silence* shows her deep concern for the need of space for females. Technically *That Long Silence* is a compact novel. Walsh in *Indian English Literature* calls it the "most technically accomplished novel" (*IEL* 117). It is more Indian, more traditional, more multicultural than any other novel written by an Indian woman writer. No western impact we detect in it and there is a credibility in the narrative account due to down-to-earth realism. However, there may be a gap between 'enacted intention' and the 'authorial intention' Dorothea Krook has taken up this aspect of intentions in the essay "Intentions and Intentions". This difference ought to be. But the fact remains that Deshpande's novel *That Long Silence* is a clarion call for half of the world's mute population to break the long silence in the succeeding days.

WORKS CITED

Deshpande, Shashi. *That Long Silence*. Delhi: Penguin India, 1989.

Gaur, Rashmi. "Female Sexuality and Introspection in Shashi Deshpande's *Moving On*" in *Indian Journal of English Studies*, ed. R.K. Dhawan, Vol. XLII (2004-2005): 31-38.

——. "Images of Indian Women in Shashi Deshpande's *That Long Silence*: Stereotypes and Realities" in *Pegasus*, ed. Usha Walter Kishore, Vol. II (Dec. 2002/Jan. 2003): 33-39.

Halperin, John. *Theory of the Novel: New Essays*. New York: Oxford University Press, 1974.

Walsh, William. *Indian English Literature*. New Delhi: Orient Longman, 1990.

3
CHAPTER

"Telling the Other Side of the Story" in Shashi Deshpande's *That Long Silence*

Veena Dwivedi

> In India, most of us find it difficult to tune in to the extreme individualism that comes to us through feminism. For instance, most women here are unwilling to assert their rights in a way that estranges them not just from their family, but also from their larger kinship group and community. (Madhu Kishwar 30-31)

The vexed familial issues underpinning traditional Indian housewives have lent narrative to many novels and movies focusing on India. An Indian housewife is expected to follow a sacrificial and torturous path in order to lead a so-called happy married life. Talking about this aspect of Indian housewives, the figures of Sita, Sati, Gandhari, among many others, come to mind immediately, as they have become an epitomé of sufferings and sacrifice in Indian history. For an Indian housewife, it is through negotiations, often accompanied with mental trauma, and corporeal sufferings, that she can write her body and manage to have some sort of existence. These themes of suffering, alienation, and existential problems dovetailed with a larger narrative about aspirations of a lonely housewife, can be registered in abundance in Shashi Deshpande's Sahitya Akedemi Winner novel, *That Long Silence* (1988). The present essay shall first examine the existential crisis in womens' lives, and then go on to show that the novel can also be studied from a gothic point of view because there exists repercussions of existential crisis and conflictual relation in the narrative of the novel.

Deshpande's *That Long Silence* (hereafter cited as *TLS*) starts off by presenting a crisis in the married life of a middle-class couple—Jaya and Mohan. Right at the very beginning, the reader is told about the existential crisis in Jaya's life, when she says, "The only memory of it that remains with me is that of fear—a fear that I was losing control over my own body" (1). Throughout the narrative, Jaya, the central character in the novel, registers the slow degeneration of her identity. She gives enough disturbing accounts of her unhappy married life, and her repeated failure to take control of her Self. Although she comes from a middle-class family, yet she aspires to have her own independent identity. It is this constant struggle, not only with her husband, Mohan, but with other members of his family (including *her* own family members) as well, that forms the background to this novel. That the novel is the story of struggle, discovery and existential problems becomes immensely apparent in the very first page of the novel when Jaya despairingly comments: "I'm writing of us. Of Mohan and me. Self-revelation is a cruel process. The real picture, the real you never emerges." This sets the story rolling as it becomes seemingly clear to readers that Jaya will be narrating the cruel life story of a 'suffering wife.' Acknowledging the resonance of this disturbed married-life throughout her cryptic story, *TLS* helps one to understand the alienation of Indian housewife against the authoritative patriarchal society. I shall now discuss how Deshpande constructs a discourse of suffering and alienation of women in this novel.

Alienation and Suffering

Jaya's life has been full of denials and negotiations. And this can be witnessed in her own statement when she says: "To know what you want...I have been denied that" (25). Deshpande presents her as a typical subaltern who "cannot speak" because she is a female, and we are all cognizant of the fact that, in the patriarchal Indian society, a woman is always looked upon as the Other—someone who needs to be groomed and looked after.

What this ostensibly means is that her freedom is curbed, and in many cases, wrongly manoeuvered by the dominating male. Jaya leads such a restricted life right from her childhood. We see that males—first her father and then her husband, Mohan—dominate her. She is denied listening to film songs by her father because he prefers classical ones. But the main crisis in the story develops when Mohan is caught up in a scandal related to a tender, in his office that threatens his job. Consequently, an inquiry has been set up against him, and it makes his married life more disturbed than ever. The conjugal life of Jaya and Mohan has never been a happy one. In fact, it was against the wishes of Jaya that she was married to Mohan. And quite interestingly Mohan has accepted this marriage proposal because Jaya was a convent-educated girl. Whereas Mohan is a kind of person who wants to flaunt off everything—even his wife, and lead a luxurious life, Jaya's ideology of life is a totally different one. She always wants to be independent and establish her own identity. But her marriage to Mohan revivified images of "Sita following her husband in exile, Savitri dogging Death to reclaim her husband, Draupadi stoically sharing her husband's travails" (11). Arguing about this sacrificial aspect of Indian women, Madhu Kishwar writes: "[a] wife is treated not as an individual who controls her own life and assets but as herself an asset who must perform several functions" (17). This is exactly what happens in the novel because Mohan wants that Jaya must acknowledge, and hence support Mohan for his wrongdoings in his office, because according to him, she and her children have been the ones for whom he has done all this.

Problems of alienation come to the surface once Mohan leaves the house after having altercation with Jaya over the scandal. There is no information to the readers about his whereabouts until the end of the novel. Concomitantly, Jaya now gets an independent life for which she has been aspiring all her life. But quite ironically, this much-awaited phase of life turns out to be a disaster because she starts losing control over her individuality. She has become so much accustomed to be identified with Mohan that this separation creates a vacuum in her life and identity. Quite interestingly, there is a rich statement in the novel which serves as a maxim for the Indian housewives as well as for Jaya and it comes from Vanitamami, Jaya's aunt: "a husband is like a sheltering tree" (32). So once the shelter has been removed, Jaya becomes totally despaired and unprotected, and enters into an endless struggle with her own self in order to search for her own identity and the meaning of life. The only thing that she has realized years later was that "you have to keep the tree alive and flourishing, even if you have to water it with deceit and lies" (32). It is not wrong, then, to agree with the critic Nancy Ellen Batty's incisive comment on the nature of relationship depicted in the novel that "the more intimate and sheltered the relationship, the more potential there is for the sense of alienation and aloneness" (111). Although, as readers, we do not witness *any* kind of intimacy between Jaya and Mohan, because theirs was a kind of relationship which existed *only* to fulfil the obligations of society, as far as Jaya's stance towards this marriage was concerned. Her deep sense of anguish in this relationship comes out vividly when she says that "I was conscious of having being chained to [Mohan's] dream" (90) and further that "The contact, the coming together, had been not only momentary, but wholly illusory as well. We had never come together, only our bodies had done that" (98). And to cite one more such instance which Jaya recalls at the end of the novel: "We lived together but there had been only emptiness between us" (185). It is in this regard that one can read contemptuous statement of the critic, Yasmin Hussain that "Women are often projected in Indian women's fiction as trapped in the categories of wife, mother and daughter. These women are usually depicted as victims of social and political injustice, cruelty and exploitation" (55). Deshpande follows the same narrative track in order to expose the traumas faced by Indian housewives within their domestic sphere. She gives us an almost similar suppressing patriarchal structure underpinning Indian housewives when Jaya recalls:

> But for the women the waiting game starts early in childhood. Wait until you get married. Wait until your husband comes. Wait until you go to your in-laws' home. Wait until you

> have kids. Yes, ever since I got married, I had done nothing but wait. (30)

It is not only Jaya who undergoes pain and sufferings but also many other female characters in the novel. For example, Jeeja, the maidservant in Jaya's house, faces corporeal sufferings at the hand of her drunkard husband. Her inability to deliver a child results in the remarriage of her husband with another woman. This again proves that a woman who fails to bear children is complicitly looked upon as an incomplete woman since she has not performed her most important bodily and earthly function. The famous Indian psychologist, Sudhir Kakkar, reflects upon this aspect of Indian society thus:

> Hindu society is of course not unique in revering motherhood as a moral, religious, or even artistic ideal, but the absolute and all encompassing social importance of motherhood, the ubiquitous variety of motherhood myths, and the function of offspring in ritual and religious (not to mention economic) life all give to motherhood in Indian culture a particularly incontrovertible legitimacy. (1981: 78)

It thus becomes apparently clear that women have no right over their bodies or roles in Indian society. They always have to adapt to the testing demands of the male. It is the male who (de)constructs the female. As Jyoti Puri has argued in her book, *Woman, Body, Desire in Postcolonial India,* "if marriage is where women are able to be sexual persons, then it is probable that sexuality would be seen as a central aspect of the marital relationship" (116). Jeeja, too, is one such victim whose failure to stand the test of her sexuality by delivering a child concomitantly results in the loss of her husband. And her suffering doesn't end here, as Rajaram, her stepson, also behaves in the same dominating manner and beats his wife, Tara, regularly. When Tara complains to Jaya about the beastly behavior of her husband, and prays for his death, Jaya retorts saying, "Stop that! Don't forget, he keeps the *kumkum* on your forehead. What a woman is without that?" (53). Here is yet again an incidence when the body of a female is written by a male, as if the woman has absolutely no control over it. It is in this context that Jasbir Jain contends that "all definitions of [feminity in India] begin with the body, its visibility and invisibility, its cycle of development and its sphere of use" (104). Jaya's revelation to her friend, Mukta, further confirms the above argument:

> All these years I thought I was Mohan's wife; now he tells me I was never that, not really. What am I going to do? What shall I do if he doesn't come back? Mukta, I was so confident, so sure of myself, I felt superior to others.... Kusum, yes, and you too...and now, without Mohan, I'm...! don't know what I'm. (185)

This revelation incisively tells us how the body of the woman is Othered. Her identity can never be complete without her partner. She needs a man who can construct and position her in the domestic sphere and society.

Interestingly, the alienation of all these female characters in the novel is undergirded by a commonality of suffering and withdrawal from their husbands—a prototype of Indian housewife. In this context, Chanda, Ho and Mathai comment: "This concept of womanhood is an eminently patriarchal construct and emphasizes suffering and duty and silence. And Jaya's universe is replete with women who subscribe to this notion of womanhood: her neighbour, her domestic servants, Mohan's mother, his sister" (1997: 61). In order to have a clear understanding of their present crisis, Deshpande weaves a narrative which consists of many flashbacks. In so doing she provides many vital past incidents related to the female characters' lives to her readers. It is a kind of labyrinth which Deshpande advertently creates and concomitantly puts a heavy demand on its readers to reconnect all the past incidents in order to have a proper understanding of the present crisis and alienation in their lives. Alienations, as we all know, are created by gaps, absences, and sometimes, even silences. Deshpande touches upon all these issues in order to allow her readers to navigate through the rough terrain of Jaya's alienation. I shall now move on to discuss the issue of silences in Jaya's life that dilapidates her individual as well as collective identity.

Silence and Domestic Terror

I have already discussed in detail how Jaya and other female characters suffer enormously throughout the novel. I shall now move on to analyse the presence of gothic elements in the novel, and in my analysis, I shall be examining Ellen Nancy Batty's recent scholarship on Deshpande's works. The neat dichotomy of subject and object which surfaces, time and again, in *TLS,* only magnifies the degree of thrill and suspense in readers' mind, making them ponder as to what will happen if the secret comes out, and it is the presence of these crypts which problematises any existing relationship in the story. The issue which I shall now undertake is how the silences over their disturbed conjugal and familial lives further contribute to their mental distress. These silences play a vital role in creating a psychological disorder in the women characters' lives. They act as a kind of what Ellen Batty terms as 'gothic' elements in the story. The term gothic can at once be seen as something which has the capacity to evoke terror and horror in one's mind. Now the question that follows is that if the novel is a narrative of domestic and conjugal problems of middle and low class Indian families, then to what extent, if any, can they evoke terror or horror? Quite interestingly, critics, as Batty argues in her brilliant book, *The Ring of Recollection,* have amazingly failed to notice this grain in Deshpande's works. If gothic is, what Tabish Khair terms in his very interesting book, *The Gothic, Postcolonialism and Otherness,* "a writing of Otherness", then *TLS* surely qualifies to be viewed as a gothic novel. I agree with this meticulous observation of Batty in regard to her arguments made regarding *TLS,* and with Khair's about gothic genre in general, because the theme of gothic runs throughout the novel as the story continuously shares a preoccupation with the Other. Here in the novel, the Otherness that one comes across operates, at once, on two levels. We see that it is not only the woman who is the Other for the man, but conversely, the same stands true for the man as well. Both man and woman in the novel are in a continual disturbing engagement with each other, as they fail to understand each other. The fear of this failure produces a silence not only in the lives of women characters, but also in the lives of male characters, like Mohan and his son Ravi.

Here in this novel, the element of gothic operates through human relationship—humans who are relentlessly caught up against the adversities of life, and hence are presented as "lonely", "confused", "helpless", "chained", "treacherous" and "silent". The novel chronicles a weird kind of human relationship which can be secured only through silence. Does this mean that Deshpande is lambasting the very idea of relationship in Indian society? The answer to this perplexing question can be found in the words of Deshpande herself. Listen to what she says in one of her interviews with Chandra Holm: "[w]e are all alone. In this world where we think that relationships are important, when we come to the roots we are alone, always alone" (8). This statement alarmingly puts the very idea of human existence in question. And because Deshpande puts all her characters in testing situations, where, their only liberation possible is through silence, and not action. And it is this loneliness that pervades almost every character in the novel. This does not mean that Deshpande is advocating passivity in life, but rather what she is suggesting is the thick cloud surrounding Indian women. To say, then, that the very term relationship between male and female acts as object of fear would not be an exaggeration. One such incidence can be witnessed in the novel where Jaya bluntly criticizes the society for viewing the man-woman relationship as something very natural. She condemns thus: "'The relation of man and woman is the most natural of one person to another.'/ Natural? 'There's only treachery, only deceit, only betrayal'" (158).

Speaking about this gothic element in the novel, Ellen Batty cites a very strong passage from Eve Kosofsky Sedgwick's book, *The Coherence of Gothic Conventions*. I shall also revert to it in order to substantiate not only my claim for viewing *TLS* as a gothic novel but, most importantly, to highlight the repercussions of Sedgwick's philosophy in Deshpande's writings. Sedgwick writes about the Self/Other problems thus:

> The self and whatever it is that is outside have a proper, natural, necessary connection to each other, but one that the self is suddenly incapable of making. The inside life and the outside life have to continue separately, becoming counterparts rather than partners, the relationship between them one of parallels and correspondences rather than communication. This, though, it may happen at an instant, is a fundamental reorganization, creating a doubleness where singleness should be.... The barrier between the self and what should belong to it can be caused by anything and nothing: but only violence or magic, and both of a singularly threatening kind, can ever succeed in joining them again. (13-14)

And it is very well known that once an object of fear is constructed, it starts acting slowly yet constantly at the psychological level producing many forms of terrors and horrors in (un)conscious state of an individual. As Fredric Jameson brilliantly argues about the gothic genre:

> Gothics are ultimately a class fantasy (or nightmare) in which the dialectic of privilege and shelter is exercised: your privileges seal you off from other people, but by the same token they constitute a protective wall through which you cannot see, and behind which therefore all kinds of envious forces may be imagined in the process of assembling, plotting, preparing to give assault. (289)

We register a constant narrative about Otherness in the novel where the characters struggle for their identity and individuality due to silences. For example, when Jaya realises that she has become "almost the stereotype of a woman: nervous, incomplete, needing male help and support" (76), and further, when she talks about Mohan: "Yes, I had always been apprehensive of not pleasing him as a woman" (96).

There is clearly a demarcation of dos and don'ts for women characters in the novel which inevitably means that throughout the novel the characters struggle to understand their roles and identity. There are rich passages in the novel which intensify the grammar of relationship. For example, when Jaya momentarily becomes aware of her duties as a wife of Mohan: "Later, when I knew him better, I realized that to him anger made a woman 'unwomanly'", and further, "I had learnt other things too, though much slowly, less painfully. I had found out the things I could do and couldn't do, all the things that were womanly and unwomanly" (83). These are interesting self-reflective statements which indicate to the disproportionate role of men in carrying on the conjugal relationship, and the onus is passed on to women to change and adapt. As Pierre Hyat argues about this aspect of relationship that "the *I* does not put itself in question; it is put in question by the other" (xiii). In the same vein, we see that women in Deshpande's world have to prove themselves to be women because their identity is put in question by the pressing demands of the male counterparts. The famous Indian critic, Meenakshi Mukherjee, reflects on this situation thus:

> Social realism at its best conveys in concrete and specific terms the complex relationships between individuals and their society. This relationship can be studied in sharper focus when the individual's life is hedged in by an enclosed space which permits very few options, and when the odds are against her, in other words, when she is a woman. (99)

This is exactly the kind of marriage institution that can be easily found in Indian society, especially the middle class. Deshpande thus tries to criticize this very system of marriage in India which operates at the cost of liberation of women, and eventually fills their lives with endless horrors. Speaking about the same issue, Ellen Batty astutely argues that: "the female protagonist in many of Deshpande's novels is quite often haunted not only by her own memories—of both childhood and marriage—but by those of her husband as well. It is as though, in re-writing her own (s)crypt and reclaiming a limited kind of agency, Deshpande's protagonist must confront or at least imagine the (s)crypt of the other that also haunts her and the marital relationship" (115).

Having argued about the theme of Otherness and Gothic elements in general, I shall now move on to examine the incidences in novel which reflect the silence of women, and the ensuing psychological distress and horror. We register a very disturbing incident when Jaya recalls the sad demise of Mohan's mother, Avva, and his sister, Vimala. Both these women die because they could never speak of the pain and suffering they underwent due to the disease. If the reason of death was the furtive abortion in Avva's case, then in the case of Vimala it was her amazing silence about her ovarian tumour. Quite interestingly, their silence is looked upon, not as despair, by Mohan and others who figure in the story, but as act of strength. The story of *TLS* is replete with such silences. Almost every character in the story has a secret to hide from the other, and it is *this* very fear of the secret getting exposed that creates a high degree of horror and fear in the characters' lives.

Mohan, too, prefers to maintain a perfect silence when it comes to his parents and family. He doesn't want that anybody, not even his wife, Jaya, should come to know about his past life. He is so much ashamed and horrified of any secrets being disclosed about his parents that at times he just brusquely makes Jaya silent whenever she makes any such inquiry. In fact, he even condemns Jaya for publishing a story, in a magazine, related to a disturbed married life of a couple because he apprehends that people might think that the couple about which Jaya has written is none other than Jaya and Mohan. He shockingly disapproves of such an audacious move of Jaya: "How can you *reveal* us, how can you reveal our lives to the world in this way?" (emphasis mine 144).

Another lurking secret which has been constantly haunting Jaya's mind is her furtive affair with Kamat—one of his neigbours, with whom Jaya unknowingly enters into some sort of intimacy. We cannot call it exactly a love-affair, since there is no such account of any such incidence throughout the story, but what we do register is the comfort and fulfilment that Jaya felt whenever she met him. She herself acknowledges the amazing sense of ease and comfort that she gets in the company of Kamat:

> But this man...it had been a revelation to me that two people, a man and a woman, could talk this way. With this man I had not been a woman. I had just been myself—Jaya. There had been an ease in our relationship. I had never known in any other. (153)

But this is only a momentary pleasure, and as soon as Kamat is found dead Jaya leaves the room immediately, fearing that her presence might create a suspicion in her own married life. But this past is never erased from her memories, and she is deeply afraid of this secret getting exposed. This only confirms that our past never leaves us. It continues to visit and haunt us time and again, no matter how hard we try to suppress or hide it from others.

In yet another incidence of a shameful secret, the reader comes to know about Jaya's furtive abortion of her child. Although she wants to disclose this secret to Mohan, the ensuing threat to their relationship prevents her in doing so. At the same time, this silence, among many other disturbing silences, creates a rift in Jaya's conjugal relationship with Mohan, and makes her mentally distressed. Jaya prioritizes Mohan's happiness and gives up her writing career, but at the end she realizes that this, too, has not brought any smoothness in their relationship. Thus Jaya blames Mohan: "It was all Mohan's fault. I had shaped myself so resolutely to his desires all these years, yet what was I left with now? Nothing. Just emptiness and silence" (144).

We thus see that this very act of revelation can create horror, terror and anxiety in one's mind because one is always scared of reviving the shameful past events. The above-quoted passages, among many others, have all the ingredients—violence, threat, mystery, revivification of a shameful past—of what it takes to qualify for a gothic genre. The gothic genre is always accompanied with many such secrets and revelations, which, when revealed, weaken and mystify one's identity, and foreshadow the depths of hidden horror and violence, thereby creating a psychological disorder and distress in the individual's mind. As David Punter and Glennis Byron incisively comment on the gothic genre in their historical book, *The Gothic,* "but what the Gothic does is to entertain the fear or rather, to follow Burke, the terror that such an enterprise may not in fact be possible, that there is something inherent in our very mortality that dooms us to a life of incomprehension, a life in which we are forever sunk in mysteries and unable to escape from the deathly consequences of our physical form" (12).

We thus witness that the alterity of the Other, in this case, the woman, has been denied throughout the story, forcing to face a conventional logic of guilt. Women have been reduced, to stereotypes, whereas the only way to come to terms with their male partners is by adopting silence and concordance with them in every act. They are endlessly engaged with this perplexing yet highly vital question of existential problem: "How do we learn to deal with our lives in a more organized, structured manner after that separation from the addiction—or the devastation caused by a close relationship with an addict?" (5).

Conclusion

> The aim and end of all thought-processes is thus to bring about a *state of identity.... Cognitive* or *judging* thought seeks an identity with a bodily cathe-xis, *reproductive* thought seeks it with a psychical cathe-xis of one's own (an experience of one's own) [*mit einer psychischen Besetzung (eigenes Erlebnis*)]. Judging thought operates in advance of reproductive thought by furnishing it with ready-made facilitations for further associative travelling. If after the conclusion of the act of thought the indication of reality reaches the perception, then a *judgement of reality, belief*, has been achieved and the aim of the whole activity attained. (Hamilton, Online)

The above-cited passage bears a close resemblance with the underlying theme of Deshpande's *TLS*. It is, as has been argued in this essay, a meta-narrative of the process of identity formation which often goes beyond the individual's control. Although the *reality* and *belief* of one's own identity achieved, if to some degree, at the end of the story, is the one which has been nourished by the necessary requirements of the societal norms. This, then, means that no matter how hard an individual struggles to gain his/her identity, yet the crux of the matter is that the construction of identity is often in the control of others. It is a continual phenomenon where the individual is in conflictual relationship with each other. Identities and relationships are always at risk in the novel due to the lurking secrets that can break its weak thread or bond. It is in such a troubled state of mind, while anxiously awaiting the return of Mohan, that Jaya realizes the ultimate reality of her life's fate: "It's dark outside, what does it matter? I can close the windows, switch on the lights and the darkness will recede. But now I know that I could never shut out the darkness; the darkness had invaded me" (181-82). This, again, is an immensely rich passage in the novel which brings Jaya's existential problems to the brim. It also has a strong presence of gothic element as we find the protagonist in deep anguish with no cogent alternative in life. To argue that Jaya has totally become a disabled woman due to the absence of Mohan in her life would not be wrong. It is not that Jaya only wants liberation from Mohan, but what troubles even more is the fact that she seems to be locking horns with all those who are having any sort of relation with her life. Her condition has become so alarming and badgering that she earnestly desires for a liberation from all bonds of relationships, and to live a free life. The real problem, as we realize, for Jaya is her existential self. Throughout the novel she is found grappling with the issue whether she should surrender herself (as she has been doing in the past) to Mohan, or to part ways from him and establish an independent identity. Finally, the only cogent alternative available for her comes from one of the sermons of *The Bhagavad Gita* wherein Lord Krishna tells Arjun that: "I have given you knowledge. Now you make the choice. The choice is yours. Do as you desire" (192). And the choice which Jaya makes is again one of denials and negotiations because she cannot bear the loss of her family.

WORKS CITED

Batty, Nancy Ellen. *The Ring of Recollection: Transgenerational Hunting in the Novels of Shashi Deshpane*. Rodopi, 2010.

Chanda, Geetanjali Singh, EY Lin Ho and K. Mathai. "Women in 'India': Four Recent Novels", *Wasafiri* (1977): 58-62.

Hamilton, Judith. "Project for a Scientific Technology." Online: http://www.judithhamiltonmd.ca/Teaching-Notes-Freud-s-Project.html (Accessed on 12 March 2013).

Holm, Chandra. "A Writer of Substance", Interview, *Indian Review of Books*, 16 May-15 June, 2000: 5-9.

Hussain, Yasmin. *Writing Diaspora: South Asian Women, Culture, and Ethnicity*. Ashgate, 2005.

Hyat, Pierre. 'Preface' in Emanuel Levinas's *Alterity and Transcendence*. Trans. Michael B. Smith. London: The Athlone Press, 1999.

Jameson, Fredric. *Postmodernism, Or, the Cultural Logic of Late Capitalism*. Duke University Press, 1991.

Kakkar, Sudhir. *The Inner World: A Psycho-Analytic Study of Childhood and Society in India*. New Delhi: OUP, 1978 (1981 ed.).

Kishwar, Madhu. *Off the Beaten Track: Rethinking Gender Justice for Indian Women*. New Delhi: Oxford University Press, 1999: 272.

——. "Rethinking Dowry Boycott." *Manushi* (September-October 1988), No. 48: 10-13.

Mukherjee, Meenakshi. *Realism and Reality: The Novel and Society in India*. New Delhi: OUP, 1991.

Punter, David and Glennis Byron. *The Gothic*. Malden: Wiley Blackwell, 2004.

Puri, Jyoti. *Woman, Body, Desire in Post-colonial India*. London & New York: Routledge, 1999.

Sedgwick, Eve Kosofsky. *The Coherence of Gothic Conventions*. London & New York: Routledge, Kegan and Paul, August 1986.

4
CHAPTER

Breaking the Barriers: A Study of Shashi Deshpande's *That Long Silence*

Sanjana Shamshery

> As I burrowed through the facts, what I found was the woman who had once lived here. Mohan's wife. Rahul's and Rati's mother. Not myself. But what was that 'myself'? Trying to find 'oneself'—what a cliché that has become. As if such a thing is possible. As if there is such a thing as one self, intact and whole, waiting to be discovered. On the contrary, there are so many, each self-attached like a Siamese twin to a self of another person, neither able to exist without the other.[1]

That Long Silence won for Shashi Deshpande the prestigious Sahitya Akademi Award in 1989. The title of the novel was inspired by the speech of Elizabeth Robins to WWSL in 1907: "If I were a man and cared to know the world I lived in, I almost think it would make me a shade uneasy—the weight of that long silence of one-half the world."[2] The novel telling the theme of a married woman who comes to terms with herself and the life around her makes the reader a shade uneasy and "will change lives" of many.[3] The complex thematic and structural pattern of the novel elevates it from a simple woman's tale of woe and misery to that of a sensitive person confronted with certain unavoidable existential problems.

The novel evokes the atmosphere in a typical Maharashtrian-Brahmin household in post-Gandhian period where film-music was tabooed and, in absence of T.V., Cinema held great fascination. Even Jaya doesn't want to miss the advertisements preceding a film. The novel is dotted here and there with the childhood memories of the protagonist Jaya of her maternal grandmother's family of Ambegaon and paternal grandmother's family at Saptagiri. Commenting on the novel, Adele King writes that the novel is definitely "Deshpande's finest novel...because it analyses emotions within rather unexceptional situations and because it creates more detailed pictures: of an extended family with its odd misfits, its petty bickerings over money, its jealousy over affections; and of a marriage in which there is no right or wrong".[4]

The yarn of the narrative is woven around Jaya, whose seventeen years of happily married life and whose dream of a bright future get imperilled owing to her husband's malpractices at his office. Their temporary shifting to the Dadar flat from the Churchgate residence in order to avoid any enquiries bestowed Jaya with an opportunity to break her humdrum household routine and to reflect upon her married life and the tension and alteration that it had brought about in her personality and 'self'. To her own bewildering shock, she discovered a wide chasm in her 'self', between what she was before marriage and what she has become after marriage:

> I'm scared of cockroaches, lizards, nervous about electrical gadgets, hopeless at technical matters, lazy about accounting ...how did I get this way? I'm sure I wasn't always like this. I can remember a time when I was not so full of fears, when the unknown, when darkness and insects did not terrify me, so when did the process of change begin? (76)

She had now to grope for an answer. Analysing the novel, Sarla Palkar writes that it "traces Jaya's passage through a plethora of self-doubts, fears, guilt, smothered anger and silence towards articulation and affirmation".[5]

Jaya's family comprising her husband Mohan, a daughter Rati and a son Rahul is a perfect ideal family like the one to be seen in glossy coloured advertisements. Beneath this shining and smooth surface is that stagnant life full of ennui and boredom resulting from a mundane routine and a "ground-swell of frustration in the married life of the protagonist who failed to be closer to her husband mentally".[6] The torpidity in Jaya's life is so deep that she is prepared to welcome any activity, howsoever disastrous it might be. Regarding Jaya's suffocated and drab life, Madhu Singh comments as follows:

> An atmosphere of apathy and boredom is created, where one can understand why Jaya should wait for "a disaster" of her own.[7]

The awareness of the coming catastrophe upon her seemingly happy family, due to Mohan's malpractices at the office, rejuvenated Jaya's sinking spirits, and she regarded it as a "prized packed, neatly tied with coloured ribbons, a gift to me from my husband" (4). She is jolted out of her hibernation, in which she has fallen after marriage. The leaves of her memory-book fluttered freely shedding the dust accumulated during the seventeen years of her marriage, so that she could read every event of her past life—her parental family at Saptagiri, her maternal family at Ambegaon; her experiences as a girl-child; above all, her delicately balanced conjugal life, her fears to lose her husband, and difficulties to deal with her growing children; and her failure as a writer. Commenting on the scarcity of the outer action in this novel and in Jai Nimbkar's *A Joint Venture* (1988), Shama Futehally writes that "there is no real story, in either novel. Yes, things do happen, but, like the discovery of Mohan's dishonesty, they are more an excuse for the introspection than anything else".[8] In her Dadar flat, Jaya confronts the ghost of Kusum (her mad cousin), Makarandmama (who presented this flat to Kusum), Kamat (Jaya's neighbour in Dadar), and her own old 'self'. The flat, thus, becomes a symbol of her roots and her past. All her feelings surface spontaneously as the hectic pattern of her daily drudgery stops in her flat in Dadar and she has "a queer sense of homecoming" (25).

"The reader goes on a roller coaster ride on the turbulent stream of narrator's consciousness."[9] Jaya is distressed over the metamorphosis that has overtaken her during the past few years. What are the reasons for this sea-change? All her experiences as a wife flash before her memory in a jiffy and she recalls the time when she had decided to tie herself in the nuptial cord with Mohan. She wonders that her marriage is based on such fragile foundations.

Jaya marries Mohan because her elder brother wants to be free from his responsibility for an unmarried younger sister, and hence he dexterously corners his sister to such a position that she is left with no other option but to marry Mohan. Other reasons forcing Jaya to marry Mohan are that he is a "soft-spoken, decent chap" (92), faircomplexioned (while Jaya is wheatish), and is working as a Junior Engineer in the New Steel Plant at Lohanagar. Moreover, he makes no demands for dowry. Under these circumstances, she thinks:

> ...If there had been no reason why I should have married Mohan, there had been not reason not to marry him either. (93)

On the other hand, Mohan marries Jaya because he wants to marry a girl who can speak "good English" (90). He is not hankering after dowry, but he wants just "an educated and a cultured wife" (90). Thus, for Mohan also, love or liking is not the touch-stone to marry Jaya; it is only a fascination for an English-speaking wife that persuades him to marry her. Since Jaya is convent-educated, Mohan thinks that his childhood dream has come true. The marriage between Jaya and Mohan is a necessity on Jaya's part—as she intends to lessen the burden on her parental family, and on Mohan's part it is merely a fulfilment of his dream. Thus, the marriage has already lost the essential complementary quality, and the basis of this marriage is not love but 'necessity' and 'fascination'. As Seema Suneel opines, the marriage "becomes more of a compromise than a relationship based on love or mutual understanding. There grows a silence between the husband and the wife."[10] How can a marriage with such weak motifs satisfy a man and a woman who enter into it under certain compulsions? The result is a great dissimilarity in their outlook upon life, with lack of communication between the two right from the day of their marriage. Neither of the couple tries to understand each other fully, and they act as total strangers in their sexual act:

> It was then that I discovered what it was all about—the songs, the poems, the stories. This I'd thought, feeling his heavy, damp body on mine, this is the real truth. (95)

Analysing the theme of the novel, the *New Society* has rightly applauded it as "a finely drawn, diaphanous portrayal of endemic imbalance in marriage...."[11] The iciness in their marital relations has frozen the natural development of the respective 'selves' of Mohan and Jaya. Incident after incident follows to shatter the 'self' of Jaya into pieces. She has to shelve her genuine feelings for the sake of Mohan. Through her stream-of-consciousness, we can candidly conjure up the moments that splinter her whole being. Jaya is renamed Suhasini after her marriage. Thus, she already has a split in her 'self'—one name stands for victory and the other symbolises submission. She comes to think thus:

> And I was Jaya. But I had been Suhasini as well. I can see her now, the Suhasini who was distinct from Jaya, a soft, smiling, placid, motherly woman. A woman who nurtured her family. A woman who coped. (15-16)

Jaya remembers her 'first quarrel'—an eye-opener as it has proved to her later on—with Mohan after their marriage. Mohan gets furious because Jaya has called his mother a 'cook' (though not a lie) and she has met his anger very deliberately. But she has not expected any harmful results. She thinks, "It was I who had left that alone after the day when my first disastrous foray into verbalising emotions had almost ripped our marriage apart" (116). Mohan assumes a silence that unnerves Jaya; her violent conduct has 'shattered' him. The conclusion is that Mohan is a traditional male chauvinist hoping a female to be submissive, and "to him anger made a woman unwomanly" (83). Her emotions make her 'ugly' in the eyes of Mohan. Thereafter, she takes greater care in displaying openly her deepest feelings to him because she is now no more 'ignorant' and 'naive': "I had learnt to control my anger after that, to hold it on a leash...I had found out all the things I could and couldn't do, all things that are womanly and unwomanly. It was when I first visited his home that I discovered how sharply defined a woman's role was" (83). Commenting on the condition of Jaya, Sarabjit K. Sandhu rightly writes thus:

> All this certainly doesn't show a natural and harmonious relationship between the two when we see that one is unable to express his or her feelings to the other.[12]

In her self-annhilating endeavour to carry on her delicately balanced married life, Jaya not only 'silences' her genuine emotions but also assumes the role of a submissive and docile wife, now no more intending to hurt her husband's feelings. Like a true traditional wife, every minute she reels under the fear of not satiating Mohan physically. She follows precisely the suggestions appearing in women-magazines for housewives how to become perfect and ideal. She follows them like the 'Bible' (96). Highlighting the altruistic gestures of the female protagonists of Deshpande's novels for their husbands, Adele King remarks:

> Shashi Deshpande's middle class Indian woman narrator is basically like the female voice described by Claudine Herrmann and other French feminist critics; she does not place herself in the centre of a universe of her own making, but rather is always painfully aware of the demands and needs of others.[13]

Similarly, Jaya being worried about the 'satisfaction' of her husband forgets to do justice to her own being. In her Dadar flat, she feels a craving for companionship even after her marriage. She painfully realizes that the physical contact is not enough for a couple for 'coming together' (98), and that their souls should be in harmony with each other. Like Maya, the central character in Anita Desai's *Cry, The Peacock* (1963), Jaya yearns for an intellectual communion with her husband, who is now leading an altogether different plane of existence.

The novel deals with the 'silence' Jaya assumes in her marital relations as well as the 'silences' of other women characters therein. Mohan's mother remained 'silent' to the numerous cruelties inflicted on her by her drunkard husband and died in silence. Similarly, Mohan's sister Vimla died without telling anybody about her suffering—she was ailing from an ovarian tumour. Kusum, Jaya's cousin, annihilated her personality in silence by committing suicide. The word 'silence' is often repeated to convey an atmosphere that allows no questioning but sitting silently despite the need to voice various injustices done to the protagonist and other minor characters. The novelist uses the term 'silence' in various contexts in the novel:

1. So many subjects were barred that the *silence* seemed heavy with uneasiness. (27)
2. Mohan and I sat together in uneasy *silence.* (27)
3. He saw strength in the woman sitting *silently* in front of the five. (36)
4. She sank into a coma and died a week later, her *silence* intact. (39)
5. The last few months there had been *silence* in his room. (49)
6. But it is he who breaks the *silence.* (188)
7. I've to erase the *silence* between us. (192)

Discussing the theme of silence in this novel, Dr. T.N. Dhar opines that "Silence, in fact, turns into a charged metaphor for female destiny because it implies acceptance of her role without complaining: to grow, to get married,...to accept the husband like a sheltering tree".[14]

Jaya is a writer and Deshpande has made this writer character convincing which many contemporary authors could not do. Her literary sensibility displays itself now and then during her thought process. We see her quoting Daniel Defoe, *The Mahabharata*, chorus in Greek Tragedy, Sonia's exhortation to Raskolnikov to kiss the earth and beg forgiveness, Fenny Prince and Aunt Bertram, and the famous story of Sister Sparrow and the Crow. We concur with Vimala Rama Rao when she writes thus:

> Jaya is one of the narrative voices in Indian English Fiction who possesses and displays literary sensibility commensurate with her own story; one whose college education and reading habits are in evidence in her speaking voice. This is indeed an achievement.[15]

Not only Jaya's being is smouldering slowly under the consecutive stress of an unbalanced married life (where there is no room for her emotions), but her writing career is also in jeopardy as it lacks the necessary impetus for such literary pursuits. Like her life, her writings become devoid of emotions. As Sarabjit K. Sandhu puts it, "This unhappiness is reflected not only in her conjugal life, but also in social life. Her books, her stories lack anger and emotion."[16] Probing into the reasons that pull her 'self' down to pieces, Jaya recollects a day in her married life which crushes her fervour for creative writing to a great extent. Jaya is joyous over her story winning a prize in a contest and getting published in a magazine. But her ecstatic moment melts away as soon as she notices some discomfiture on Mohan's countenance. She expects him to share her happiness instead of getting "hurt" (144). When Jaya enquires about his uneasiness, Mohan replies "How can you reveal us, how can you reveal our lives to the world in this way?" (144). Jaya's jocund mood recedes at the indifference of her husband over her success. She then thinks as follows:

> I had known then that it hadn't mattered to Mohan that I had written a good story, about a couple, a man who could not reach out to his wife except through her body. For Mohan it had mattered that people might think the couple was us, that the man was him. To Mohan, I had been no writer, only an exhibitionist. (144)

Commenting on the dilemma of the tradition-bound, modern woman to be found in the novels of Shashi Deshpande, B.K. Das writes thus:

> Through Jaya's character Shashi Deshpande has thus expressed the ambivalent attitude of contemporary educated independent minded Indian women who can neither reconcile themselves to a new situation when their husbands ignore them and crush their ambition in life nor cast off their husbands simply because the husband is like a sheltering tree they cannot afford to live without.[17]

The deadly 'silence' that she maintains as her weapon in marital relations hinders her from expounding to Mohan that her story has not arisen from any actual experience. She, therefore, adopts silence, lest she should displease him. After this episode, she stops writing stories temporarily, as she herself puts it:

> I had relinquished them instead, all those stories that had been taking shape in me because I had been scared—scared of hurting Mohan, scared of jeopardising the only career I had, my marriage. (144)

Jaya has *de riqueur* 'silenced' her desires, ambitions, and her writing capacities for the satisfaction of her husband. Since she cannot suppress her penchant for writing for long, she starts writing again stalkingly. She has dumped her rejected stories in the Dadar flat without letting Mohan know about them.

Because of the tense and unhappy conjugal relations, Jaya is slowly yet steadily losing sight of the "personal vision" (147)—a thing essential for the success of a writer. All her stories are rejected by the editors of various magazines. One day, utterly disappointed by the repudiation of her one more story, Jaya goes straight to Kamat (her neighbour, with whom Jaya has evolved some sort of friendship), and compels him to read her story and point out the errors. Kamat concludes evaluatingly:

> ...I'll tell you what's really wrong with your story. It's too restrained. Spew out your anger in your writing, woman, spew it out. Why are you holding it in? (147)

Now, for the second time again, Jaya feels that anger makes a woman 'unwomanly', and so she suppresses it in her personal life as well as in her literary genius, thus gradually relegating her whole 'self' to non-entity: "A woman can never be angry; she can only be neurotic, hysterical, frustrated" (147). Here Jaya's malaise assumes a universal dimension and projects the torment of the Indian housewives who have to smash the shackles of an orthodox tradition before enterprising into the arena of a competitive professional career. As Anjali Yardi remarks, "...it is the particular strength of the realistic novel to evoke through its picture of a few individual lives, a sense of a whole milieu, its ethos and ambience, its physical and social environment."[18] The reason that Kamat attributes to Jaya's failure as a writer is her fear of hurting Mohan, who feels perturbed thinking that her stories contained material from their personal lives; secondly, she is also 'scared of failing', of being rejected by editors. She, therefore, starts writing "humorous pieces about the travails of a middleclass housewife" (148-49), whose name is "Seeta". In this way, she suppresses the voice of her being in order to please Mohan and various editors:

> ... I had shut the door, firmly, on all those other women who had invaded my being, screaming for attention; women I had known I could not write about, because they might—it was just possible—resemble Mohan's mother, or aunt, or my mother or aunt. Seeta was safer. (149)

Kamat, a true well-wisher of Jaya, feels greatly annoyed on seeing her trying at such trivial themes. He calls her story "Seeta" her 'obnoxious creation'. This time Jaya pays no heed to Kamat's criticism as her humorous pieces neither offend her husband nor invite any rebuff from editors. On the other hand, they satiate her creative mind to some extent. At this point, we may draw a major conclusion that it is her conjugal life that plays havoc with her creative capacities, adding one more fatal twist to her already deteriorating 'self'.

Jaya's strained marital alliance due to lack of communication with Mohan along with her exigency to regain her alienated 'self' lures her to the embalming company of Kamat, who is also a victim of loneliness. She often meets him as he is her neighbour at Dadar flat. In Kamat Jaya finds a full scope for good friendship and a person with whom she can discuss her writings and personal problems. Her literary intellect that is slowly heading towards numbness in gelid surroundings of her husband's house, gets rejuvenated in the warm company of Kamat. She remembers her relationship with Kamat as follows:

> With this man I had not been a woman. I had been just myself—Jaya. There had been an ease in our relationship. I had never known in any other. There had been nothing I could not say to him. And he too.... (153)

And further:

> I told him things I'd never been able to speak of, not to Dada, not to Mohan. (153)

Moreover, she gets a sort of father-like protection from Kamat. J. Bhavani propagates our idea when he says that Naren in *Roots and Shadows* and Kamat in *That Long Silence* are "wise father surrogates who can support them [the heroines] in their endeavour".[19] They are the persons who are in full control of their lives and therefore can guide others also in search of their 'selves'. Once swayed by nostalgic memories of her father, Jaya weeps vehemently in front of Kamat and he comforts her. This gesture of Kamat makes her feel "like wearing Appa's coat on a chilly night, like sitting before him on his bike" (156). But Jaya's "pursuit of happiness" (156) takes her too far in her association with Kamat and it soon starts growing physical. Though Jaya has resisted her corporeal desires, she never resents Kamat's advances towards her. Rather, she seems to relish them, as she also 'responds' to him with equal gusto. Perhaps the every consciousness that she need not 'silence' her emotions with Kamat during love-making as she has to do with Mohan decoys Jaya into such a relationship. Jaya's relations with Kamat might have assumed sexual dimensions, had he not died all of a sudden. The incident of his death is like a bolt from the blue for Jaya, as it makes her see her own misdirected strides. The pillar on which she is resting her hopes of finding her 'self' and happiness has splintered into pieces unexpectedly and abruptly. She remembers the time of Kamat's death thus:

> But after his death, nothing between me and Mohan either. We lived together but there bad been only emptiness between us. (185)

Once more Jaya is left lonely and dry in the vast shoreless sea of life. Later, she tries to assess her relationship with Kamat as follows:

> And yet I knew I had to puzzle it out, to put the bits and pieces together and see what form it took, my relationship with this man. (185)

Possibly their relationship could not put on a concrete form due to the sudden expiry of Kamat.

Jaya's revolting being that rejuvenates in intimate companionship of Kamat recedes into a calm and hypocritical delight in her married life. She again plunges into the pit of loneliness and selflessness. But the lack of communication with her husband further deepens and she is left in a state of utter confusion and claustrophobia:

> I had shaped myself so resolutely to his desires all these years, yet what was I left with now? Nothing. Just emptiness and silence. (144)

The shackles of tradition fall heavily on Jaya, and she can't show the essence of her 'real being'. As a consequence, she tries to destroy an unborn child of Mohan without his knowledge. Moreover, she has established a kind of physical relationship with Kamat, dodging Mohan to a large extent. After some true heart-searchings, she decides to shun these lies and deceits, for no marriage can survive for long on such fragile foundations.

Jaya comes to address herself to Mohan's needs and moods, and in the process she loses sight of her emotional and intellectual requirements. Shorn of any real purpose in life, Jaya is drawn to melancholia and solitude. Even "the diverse sounds of Bombay" seem to her "an endless assault on the ears" (56). The chaotic milieu of Bombay projects the mental upheaval of the heroine herself. Jaya confesses at one place:

> Almost worse to me than this...had been the sense of being invaded, not just by sounds, but by a multitude of people and their motions as well. Anger, fear, hatred, envy, tenderness, love, all of these came to me as I lay in bed, a fascinated listener. (56)

Each stirred emotion within her is actually an 'invasion' on her hypersensitive being. This quality of 'secludedness' is a universal characteristic of all the heroines of Deshpande. In this particular state of mind, they realize the essential loss of their 'selves' and set out to search for them. Similarly, the word 'alone' is a recurring phenomenon in *That Long Silence,* for example Jaya tells us time and again:

> It was a relief to be alone. I'd always treasured my hours of solitude without Mohan and the children. (68)

While Jaya is thus enmeshed between an engaging tussle emanating from her present state of loneliness and alienation, confusion and claustrophobia, she keeps on suggesting to herself: "I can't cope, I won't" (191). She procures a golden opportunity to escape from the smothering surroundings of her house at Churchgate in Bombay, but even that is washed away. Jaya reflects on her situation thus:

> My own career as a wife was in jeopardy. The woman who had shopped and cooked, cleaned; organised and cared for her home and her family with such position...where had she gone? (24-25)

Critically she analyses that she has steered the wheel of her life in a wrong direction, and the result is that there is no visible link between old Jaya and present Jaya. The main reason for this sea-change is her marriage with Mohan.

After recollecting her past life and emptying her memory-bag, Jaya tries to discover the reason for the loss of her 'self' and sets out to search for it. She says, "I had to get a grip on myself" (127). Commenting on Jaya's faculty to retrospect and rearrange the chaotic sequences of events in her life, Kamini Dinesh writes as follows:

> Her narrative is what the psychoanalyst calls "a talking cure". Though there is no analyst who disrupts the narrative, memories flood in often linked by the vaguest association of ideas and each incident, a little story in itself, gives a new perspective and recreates the speaker.[20]

Deshpande makes the Dadar flat, apart from the hearts and minds of the characters, the "battle-ground", and this imparts a "hothouse atmosphere about the novel which can get claustrophobic at times".[21] She regards herself and Mohan as a "pair of bullocks yoked together" (7) who want to assure their own ways but cannot do so because it is painful to have different ways:

> Two bullocks yoked together that was how I saw the two of us the day we came here. Mohan and I. Now I reject that image. It's wrong. If I think of us in that way, I condemn myself to a lifetime of disbelief in ourselves. I've always thought—there is only one life, no chance of a reprieve,

> no second chances. But in this life itself there are so many crossroads, so many choices. (192-93)

She now decides to be true to her own 'self'. She has found out that it is not 'love' but her 'habit of being wife' that has made her dependent on Mohan. It is not Mohan but marriage that has made her 'circumspect'. When Mohan leaves her, though temporarily, she is surrounded by all types of fears that he might leave her forever. She decides that her marriage will not depend on "deception, lies, evasions forever" (132). She resolves to "get out of this" and "get myself in hand" (137). Commenting on the transformation of Jaya, Dr. Das writes:

> The image of the woman underwent a metamorphosis when the contemporary woman decided to cast off her traditional role of living under the shade of her husband.[22]

Jaya henceforth abandons the artificial masks of an arrogant and a self-satisfied woman in order to discover her true 'self'.

A relevant question that arises at this juncture is: Why is Jaya attempting to veil her real 'self'? The much sought-after answer could be found in the following extract:

> —All of us, bound by fear. Yes, I have been scared, scared of breaking through that thin veneer of a happy family. (191)

This chimera of happiness disappears as soon as Jaya realizes that the "pursuit of happiness" is "a meaningless, unending exercise, like a puppy chasing its tail" (156). She has camouflaged her real 'self' under the cover of the nameplates of "Mohan's wife" and "Rahul's and Rati's mother" (173), but the cruel, sharp staves of reality compel her eventually to emerge from her "warm and safe hole". Consequently,

> Smugness fell away from me, not in bits and pieces, but in mammoth, frightening chunks. (174)

Her being is presently baffled by the lustre of reality, and her vision, being murky so long due to the loss of 'self', now becomes clearer by slow degrees. She, who has been oblivious of her own demands and purposes in life, catches hold of them again. She also realizes that to strengthen her collapsing married life, she will have to "erase the silence" between herself and Mohan.

The ever-yawning gulf of communication must be bridged and a harmony in their outlook upon life must be established. Earlier, Jaya had regarded her relationship with Mohan as an unavoidable impediment in achieving her true 'self', but now she comprehends the complementary role of husband and wife, and says "without Mohan, I'm—I don't know, I don't know what I am" (185). In this context, Suresh Chandra writes thus in an article:

> Both Jaya and Ainsley (the protagonist in *The Edible Woman*) appear to realize that neither is woman prisoner, nor man free because both are the constituents of the cycle of procreation and providing.[23]

Owing to the incompatibility with her husband, Jaya is inclined towards melancholy and solitude, and Mohan's presence becomes a "burden" to her. She desires an alienation from the outer world in order to think of herself and to discover the missing links in her being. Now, Jaya comprehends woefully that she has to desist from this love of solitude if she wants to bridge the communication-gap between herself and her husband and children. Ultimately, she declares her resolve thus: "I will have to speak, to listen, I will have to erase the silence between us" (193).

As the novel approaches its terminating point, we find Jaya turning over a completely new leaf of life, and her pessimistic notions towards life are superseded by optimistic ones. She now decides to express her pent-up emotions to her husband in order to be true to her 'being' and to her spouse. She comes to shun her love of solitudue and is determined to 'erase the silence' marring her cheerful domestic life. "Shashi Deshpande's protagonists find freedom not in the western sense but in conformity with the society they live in without drifting away from one's culture,"[24] says T. Ashoka Rani. Jaya is skeptical whether the family could "go back to being what we were" and whether she could 'mend' the damages done in the conjugal life. The novel winds up on a sanguine note, as Jaya anticipates a change in Mohan's attitude. Even Mohan is likely to rectify his ways, realizing the fatal effects of his malpractices on the future of the family:

> We don't change overnight. It's possible that we may not change even over long periods of time. But we can always hope. Without that; life would be impossible. And if there is anything I know now it is this: life has always to be made possible. (193)

Mohan might change or not, but Jaya has definitely transformed herself into a totally new person, and is already on her way to regain her 'self' and learns "to take the responsibility for her life".[25] David Kerr evaluating the novel writes that "Shashi Deshpande in this novel offers readers an intimate and domestic chronicle of the subtle tyrannies suffered by women and of the pain of coming to self-knowledge, or at least to the conditions which must be fulfilled before self-knowledge can be attained".[26] At the end of the novel, Jaya is reminded of a sermon of Lord Krishna to Arjuna in the *Bhagavad Gita*—"*Yathechhasi tatha Kuru*" (i.e., Do as you wish to), and her trapped soul feels fluttering like a roll of paper in the open air, which signifies her emancipation from a self-created 'prison'. Opining about this change that has overtaken Jaya, Suresh Chandra observes:

> Jaya attains '*Yathechhasi tatha kuru*' status only after she has undergone all types of emotional purgation. Worldly considerations look too petty to her now. She is a truly liberated person after realizing the man's place in the world of a woman and *vice-versa*.[27]

In her conjugal life as well as in her writing career, Jaya has accomplished that 'status' and she has finally steered the wheel of her marital life in the right direction and has "tried painfully to retrace my way back through the disorderly, chaotic sequence of events and non-events that made up my life" (187). Similarly, reflecting on the future of her writing career, Jaya at once feels like the "girl, a child, wearing a dress with pockets for the first time, thrusting her hands in them, feeling heady with the excitement of finding unexpected resources within herself" (187). This picture of her own infancy provides her with a wise clue that a person has resources within oneself. But at times one becomes oblivious of one's own faculties and wanders outside for them. In a flash, she decides to start afresh her writing career with this "child, hands in pockets" up to the elderly and resentful woman that she is by now. Perhaps the manifold meaning of the 'sermon' has 'seeped' deep into the consciousness of the protagonist, who at once throws away the yoke of fears, i.e. the fear of failing in the journalistic arena and the fear of displeasing Mohan, that are hounding her away from the practice of a genuine pencraft. The following passage from the novel highlights this point:

> What have I achieved by this writing? The thought occurs to me again as I look at the neat pile of papers. Well, I've achieved this. I'm not afraid any more. The panic has gone. I'm Mohan's wife, I had thought, and cut off the bits of me that had refused to be Mohan's wife. Now I know that kind of fragmentation is not possible. The child, hands in pockets, has been with me through the years. She is with me still. (191)

Not only the 'silence' of Jaya is broken, but other characters become vocal and expressive at the moment. Rahul, Jaya's son, tries to speak out about his problems. Jaya has put her children—Rahul and Rati—also in the 'slots' of fake happiness. They are not allowed to do what they want. Children are forced to join Rupa's family (Jaya's friend) on their trip to the South. But Rahul escapes in the middle of the tour to his Vasant Uncle. By the time he returns with his uncle, he has decided to break his 'silence' and speak out about his problems to his mother. Mohan who has never expressed his feelings openly to Jaya, starts a rapport with Jaya with all good intentions. We might regard this as a meaningful stride towards a new beginning of harmonious relationship between husband and wife, between parents and children. Sarla Palkar comments in this context that "by the end of the novel, the crisis—a mere storm in the teacup—has been averted and every thing outwardly appears to be as it had been. Except for what has happened to Jaya. Jaya can no longer be a passive, silent partner to Mohan."[28]

Shashi Deshpande deftly weaves some visual images to concretise the heroine's mental state to the reader. We don't find such remarkable imagery in her other novels. To convey the sense of compulsion pervading Jaya's marriage, Mrs. Deshpande uses the imagery of "two bullocks yoked together". Jaya and Mohan are leading their life mechanically without mutual love, which is both the sustenance and essence of marriage. Another striking example of her imagery is the image of a "worm crawling into a hole", which suggests the mental state of Jaya, a budding writer who is doomed to dwindle into a stereotyped Indian housewife.[29] A husband is compared to "a sheltering tree" by the orthodox Indian woman. He is supposed to protect the helpless woman from the hostile world around. By this image, Shashi Deshpande sketches before us the unwanted pity bestowed on the woman by men to keep an upper hand on the fair-sex. To show the docile housewife Suhasini's (*alias* Jaya's) self-satisfied existence, Deshpande gives us the fable of the cunning sparrow and the crow. Suhasini is the sparrow of the story. She sits comfortably in her house with her children thinking that as long as she is in her house she is safe from the hostile world outside. Similarly, the mythological tale of Gandhari bandaging her eyes out of love for her blind husband is used for Jaya, who despite her awareness of her husband's malpractices at office, raises no protest against them.

Thus, *That Long Silence* is a narrative depicting a woman who desires to become rebellious after years of subjugation to her husband, here she forfeits the idea for the better future of the family. Though she desists from a revolt she hopes to have a better understanding with her husband, who is equally eager to embark on a new lease of life to create a promising future for the family. Taking the overall view of the novel, Dr. K. Madhavi Menon writes in the following manner:

> Women have allowed victimization instead of bargaining for partnership.... It is not the fault of men alone that has caused the feminine discontent. A patriarchal order can be subverted If only women take their ranks in the order of intelligence and individuality.[30]

Evidently, a meaningful co-existence can come through mutual understanding and respect and not through domination and subjugation—and this is the *leit motif* of this novel.

NOTES

1. Shashi Deshpande, *That Long Silence* (1988; New Delhi: Penguin Books, 1989), 69.
2. Quoted in Shashi Deshpande's *That Long Silence.*
3. *The Evening Post* quoted on the cover page of *That Long Silence.*
4. Adele King, "Shashi Deshpande: Portraits of an Indian Woman", *The New Indian Novel in English,* ed. Viney Kirpal (New Delhi: Allied Publishers Ltd., 1990), 165-66.
5. Sarla Palkar, "Breaking the Silence: Shashi Deshpande's *That Long Silence,*" *Feminism and Recent Fiction,* ed. Sushila Singh (New Delhi: Prestige Books, 1991), 129.
6. B.K. Das, *Recent India Fiction,* ed. R.S. Pathak (New Delhi: Prestige Books, 1994), 204.
7. Madhu Singh, "Intimate and Soul-Searching Portrayals of Marriage," *Indian Book Chronicle* (July 1993), 22.
8. Shama, Futehally, "Of the Elusive Self," a Review of *That Long Silence. The Book Review,* 13, Nos. 3 & 4 (May-Aug. 1989): 30.
9. Keki N. Daruwalla, "An Intense Book", *Indian Literature,* 34, No. 6 (Nov.-Dec. 1991): 32.
10. Seema Suneel, "Shashi Deshpande, Rajendra Awasthy and Syed Abdul Malik: Life and Works", *Man-Woman Relationship in Indian Fiction* (New Delhi: Prestige Books, 1995), 24.
11. Cover page comments of the *New Society, That Long Silence.*
12. Sarabjit K. Sandhu, *The Novels of Shashi Deshpande* (New Delhi: Prestige Books, 1991), 38.
13. Adele King, "Shashi Deshpande: Portraits of an Indian Woman", *The New Indian Novel in English,* ed. Viney Kirpal, 165.
14. T.N. Dhar, "Protrait of a Marriage", *Indian Book Cltronicle,* 15, Nos. 1 & 2 (Jan.-Feb. 1990): 7.
15. Vimala Rama Rao, "A Well-Articulated Silence", *The Literary Criterion,* 27, No. 4 (1992): 76.
16. Sarabjit K. Sandhu, *The Novels of Shashi Deshpande,* 41.
17. B.K. Das, "Shashi Deshpande's *That Long Silence", Recent Indian Fiction,* ed. R.S. Pathak, 207.
18. Anjali Yardi, A review of *That Long Silence, The Indian P.E.N.,* 51, Nos. 1-3 (Jan.-March 1990): 20.
19. J. Bhavani, "Nirdvandva: Individuation and Integration as the Heroine's Quest in Shashi Deshpande's Fiction", *Indian Women*

Novelists, III, 4th ed., R.K. Dhawan (New Delhi: Prestige Books, 1995), 29.

20. Kamini Dinesh, "*That Long Silence:* The Narrator and The Narrative", *Contemporary Indian Fiction in English,* ed. Avdhesh K. Singh (New Delhi: Creative Books, 1993), 85.
21. Keki N. Daruwalla, "An Intense Book", *Indian Literature,* 34, No. 6 (Nov.-Dec. 1991): 34.
22. B.K. Das, "Shashi Deshpande's *That Long Silence,*" *Recent Indian Fiction,* ed. R.S. Pathak, 209.
23. Suresh Chandra, "Women's Liberation in the Fiction of Margaret Atwood and Shashi Deshpande", *Meerut Journal of Comparative Literature and Language,* VI, No. 2 (1993): 83.
24. T. Ashoka Rani, "Feminism *vis-à-vis* Women's Dignity: A Study of Shashi Deshpande's *That Long Silence", The Journal of Indian Writing in English,* 24, No. 1 (Jan. 1996): 21.
25. Adele King, A Review of *That Long Silence, World Literature Today*, 62, No. 4 (Aug. 1998): 727.
26. David Kerr, "History and the Possibilities of Choice: A Study of Anita Desai's *Baumgartner's Bombay*, Upamanyu Chatterjee's *English August* and Shashi Deshpande's *That Long Silence*", *Indian Women Novelists*, I.1. ed. R.K. Dhawan (New Delhi: Prestige Books, 1991): 137.
27. Suresh Chandra, "Women's Liberation in the Fiction of Margaret Atwood and Shashi Deshpande", *Meerut Journal of Comparative Literature and Language,* VI, No. 2 (1993): 84.
28. Sarla Palkar, "Breaking the Silence: Shashi Deshpande's *That Long Silence*", *Feminism and Recent Fiction,* ed. Sushila Singh, 129.
29. B.K. Das, "Shashi Deshpande's *That Long Silence* and the Question of the Reader's Response", *Aspects of Commonwealth Literature* (New Delhi: Creative Books, 1995), 128.
30. K. Madhavi Menon, "The Crisis of Feminism: Shashi Deshpande's *That Long Silence", Commonwealth Quarterly,* 18, No. 46, (Dec.-March 1993): 36.

5
CHAPTER
Breaking That Long Silence: The Quest for Space, Identity and Independence

Sthitaprajna

With her novels, Shashi Deshpande has achieved a reputation as a writer who adds a strong, unique and culturally relevant feminist voice to modern Indian English literature. She has been applauded by feminist critics for creating female characters who are able to speak and act independently and have enough sense of personal identity as they struggle, in virtual isolation, to overcome the various injustices in their domestic and social arena. These characters are mostly educated, middle-class Indian women who are financially secured and have the awareness about their rights and have the ability to speak and stand for a cause, yet,...the silence continues.

While some of her women protagonists refuge to compromise and instead create an entirely new path for themselves, some choose to deal with their problems within their own cultural setting. They are unable to completely break-free from the confines of their homes but ultimately these women make choices that make their life more meaningful and wholesome within their cultural and domestic territory. This emerges from the dilemma women face in wanting to keep traditions while at the same time, wanting to reject what, in society, ties them down. The story of Jaya, who seems to be the author's mouthpiece in *That Long Silence,* is the realistic picture of every middle-class, educated Indian woman—seemingly she has all the freedom to enjoy but she is confined between realizations and restrictions.

Jaya, the protagonist, is an educated, middle-class woman who lives with her husband Mohan and her two children, Rahul and Rati. With "Well-educated, hard-working people in secure jobs, cushioned by insurance and provident funds, with two healthy, well-fed children going to good schools" (5), what else could she ask for from life? She was a dutiful wife, an affectionate mother and was—carefully being—dutiful to her in-laws and her relatives. Mohan too was the perfect husband. The family was picture-perfect, like "a glossy, coloured advertising visual. We smiled, we laughed; I, the mother, served them with 'love and care'; Mohan, the head of the family, smiled indulgently, and the children were lively and playful" (4).

After completing her graduation, Jaya gets married to Mohan and settles down for her role as a dutiful wife to an extent that she is asked to give up her maiden name "Jaya" and assume the name "Subhasini" given by Mohan. Metaphorically, this also means losing her identity. Her father names her Jaya which means victory. But she is renamed Suhasini, a milder and more submissive one. She is twice displaced; once when she is renamed Suhasini by her husband and second when she renames herself as Seeta to pursue her writing. She has always made compromises to please her husband. She had almost assumed her identity as Mohan's wife and "cut off the bits of me that had refused to be Mohan's wife" (191).

Life becomes very predictable for her and "the illusion of happiness" that she had long woven for herself is gone. As time passed by the monotony of her schedule began taunting her and she had "to admit the truth to myself—that I had often found family life unendurable. Worse than anything else had been the boredom of the unchanging pattern, the unending monotony" (4). She realizes her husband's apathy and growing indifference towards her. He takes her for granted; and is never bothered for her emotions, likes and dislikes. To make matters worse, Mohan is accused of corruption and is under investigation. He goes in hiding for a few days and all this sets Jaya thinking. She is forced to rethink about her past in an attempt to think who she is. Her self-efficacy leads her to self-realization. She, at last strives to break her long silence and goes on to search for her identity and her individuality. As David Buckingham analyses the issue of identity, he very rightly observes:

> Globalization, the decline of the welfare state, increasing social mobility, greater flexibility in employment, insecurity in personal relationships—all these developments are contributing to a sense of fragmentation and uncertainty, in which the traditional resources for identity formation are no longer so straightforward or so easily available. Like many contemporary authors, Bauman emphasizes the fluidity of identity, seeing it as almost infinitely negotiable, and in the process perhaps underestimates the continuing importance of routine and stability. Nevertheless, his general point is well taken: "identity" only becomes an issue when it is threatened or contested in some way and needs to be explicitly asserted. (2008: 1-2)

For Jaya her identity is threatened. She is groping for an identity. When a magazine asked her a bio-data she found herself "agonizing over what I could write, what there was in my life that meant something. Finally, ...only these had remained: I was born. My father died when I was fifteen. I got married to Mohan. I have two children and I did not let a third live" (2). We find here two very pertinent issues: Jaya's problem of identity and her tendency to define herself in terms of others (someone's daughter, someone's wife, and, someone's mother). She did not have much to talk about herself. She experiences a constant conflict of being her own self and being "a good wife", "a good mother" and "a good daughter". The way in which her conflict is designed and structurally implemented reveals traditional roles delineated to each gender in Indian society. Being a patriarchical society, we have defined roles for men and women.

In some respects, Simone de Beauvoir's trenchant observation, "He is the Subject, he is the Absolute—she is the Other," sums up why the self is such an important issue for feminism. This outside is spoken of in the spirit of the Levisian 'other', an other that calls for a responsibility to its absent presence, rather than an other to be engulfed within. This can be seen in Derrida's reading of Heidegger and Nietzsche, trying to come to terms with the figure of 'woman' in *Spurs: Nietzsche's Styles:* "There is no such thing as a woman, as a truth in itself of woman in itself" (1979: 101). He goes on to say, "…If style were a man, then writing would be a woman" (1979: 57). Woman is to man what madness is to reason; "a constitutive outside, a wholly other". Considering that woman is outside the dominant discourse, she cannot speak. As Gayatri Spivak writes in her article "Can the Subaltern Speak?"

> Between patriarchy and imperialism, subject constitution and object formation, the figure of a woman disappears, not into a pristine nothingness, but into a violent shuttling which is the displaced figuration of the 'Third World Woman' caught between tradition and modernization. (1994: 102)

Traditional Indian cultural narratives are pervasive and serve to typify personal identity and experience. These cultural narratives portray Indian women as wife and mother, nurturing, obedient, forbearing, soft-spoken, and the primary transmitters of the ethnic culture. More prevalent, however, is the cultural identity of Indian woman as wife and mother, subordinate to her husband and his family, forbearing to her family, moral and obedient. These categorical identities or "formula stories" reinforce cultural expectations and perceptions of morality.

The personal narratives, of how an individual (read woman) makes sense of her life as opposed to these formula stories, have to be constantly re-created, negotiated and challenged because they do not neatly fit into these formula stories. But the foremost identity of woman is defined as a wife and mother. Cultural practices in India have always acknowledged patriarchy and the belief that men are dominant/superior to women. According to the traditional Indian cultural narrative, women are expected to maintain the home and family, and exercise unconditional self-sacrifice and nurturance. The traditional Indian female identity places women in a very restrictive role. Education, for example, is seen as a means to increase the social status of women for the purpose of finding a more desirable husband and not viewed as a tool to increase their independence or move forward in their careers. In *Femininity, Feminism and Gendered Discourse,* Janet Holmes and Meredith Marra very rightly remark:

> Assumptions about what constitute more feminine as opposed to more masculine ways of talking are constantly being reinforced in everyday interaction, and the process of "gendering" individuals is on-going and dynamic. Denying this is misleading and potentially damaging to the feminist enterprise, as we elaborate below. In the early nineteenth century, for instance, normatively feminine ways of talking entailed being largely silent in public spheres. And even after women gained the right to be heard in public contexts, they faced the consequences of a "gendered division of linguistic labour" which ensured they often found it difficult to participate on equal terms with men. Women's voices were considered by the BBC, for instance, to be "unsuitable for 'serious or symbolic occasion[s]', though acceptable in more 'frivolous' contexts". (2010: 3-4)

Good or bad, most women allow relationships to define them. Most women are scared of being alone. They get their sense of worth from being someone's wife, daughter or mother. As Jaya says: "Even a worm has a hole it can crawl into. I had mine—as Mohan's wife, as Rahul's and Rati's mother. And so I had crawled back into my hole. I had felt safe there. Comfortable, Unassailable. And so I had stopped writing" (148).

Probably Jaya stopped writing because of many reasons—because of Mohan, because of apathetic people like Laxman Kaka and most importantly because of her own fear of failing. Jaya blames everyone and everything for not writing. "I gave up my writing because of you," I said to Mohan, and he seemed astonished (143). Mohan did not appreciate Jaya on winning a prize for her story; he rather reproached her saying, "how could you, how could you have done it?... They will all know now, all those people who read this and know us, they will know that these two persons are us, they will think I am this kind of a man, they will think I am this man. How can I look anyone in the face again? And you, how could you write these things, how could you write such ugly things, how will you face people after this?" (143-44).

Jaya could never retaliate, she could never protest or resist and her creative skill was oppressed under the weight of her silence.

And the silence is so over-powering that it engulfs everything. Quoting Rajan: "The force of Deshpande's indictment of women's lines lies in the way she is able to universalize their silence, chiefly by drawing similarities among Jaya and a variety of other female figures, including characters from Indian history and myth; and among three generations of women in her family (Jaya, her mother, her grandmother); among different classes of women (Jaya, her maid Jeeja); among different kinds of women of the same class and generation (Jaya, her cousin Kusum, her widowed neighbor Mukta)" (1993: 83).

At many a time silence acts as a strong weapon of protest but for Jaya who had been silenced since her childhood silence becomes a defence mechanism. Because, as Jaya says, "a woman can never be angry; she can only be neurotic, hysterical, frustrated. There's no room for anger in my life, no room for despair either. There's only order and routine—today, I have to change the sheets; tomorrow, scrub the bathrooms; the day after, clean the fridge..." (147-48).

Silence is part of a woman discourse. Even if women want to speak out, they were always silenced. As Sara Mills writes, "the discourses which circulated within the nineteenth century around the question of women and reading are simply evidence of the great difficulty which women found in inhabiting the discursive structures laid out for them which stressed their duties and obligations as wives and mothers and did not hold out space for them to negotiate their own pleasures" (1997: 90). It becomes all the more evident by reading the following passage from Thomas Broadhurst's *Advice to Young Ladies on the Improvement of the Mind and Conduct of Life* (1810):

> She who is faithfully employed in discharging the various duties of a wife and a daughter, a mother and a friend, is far more usefully occupied than one who, to the culpable neglect of the most important obligations, is daily absorbed by philosophic and literary speculations, or soaring aloft amidst the enchanted regions of fiction and romance. (Cited in Sara Mills, 1997: 89)

Though this piece of advice may seem to be an instruction manual for the expected role of a woman which is defined to be a good wife and mother, it also discourages the behaviour a woman should not possess, in this case reading, which could prove as a detriment to her obligatory duties.

Similarly, for Jaya, she was initially encouraged to write some "light, humorous pieces about the travails of a middle-class housewife. Nothing serious..." (148-49). She writes what her husband and others want to read not what she wants to write. And when she did what she wanted to she was scorned at by Mohan, ridiculed by Laxman Kaka and dismissed by the magazine's editor as "a middle-class stuff, women's problem" (146). She did not want to "jeopardise the only career I had, my marriage" (144) by hurting Mohan. So she started writing with a false name Seeta; the chosen name quite symbolic of her conformist and conventional attitude.

The internalization of patriarchal violence for centuries is the reason why most women are unable to escape and condone some forms of physical, emotional and psychological abuse. They suffer from a depleted sense of self-esteem. They feel disempowered and it has its roots in childhood conditioning. These women never would have possibly spoken their minds or rebelled during their childhood. Like Jaya, who as child always wanted to listen to Radio Ceylon but could not because her father would always tell her, "What poor taste you have, Jaya" (3) and "The shame I had felt then survived long" (3). She could never protest against her father and she could "never dare to confess" to Mohan how much she enjoyed the ads amidst movies. The problem was she saw her father's image in her husband and never wanted to rebel. So after the father it is the husband who dominates her, unknowingly, right from the beginning of the relationship.

Moreover, the fear of losing their sense of security and the fear of uncertainty make women like Jaya get addicted to abuse. The innate fear of abandonment in Jaya does not allow her to do what she wants to. Though she is educated and empowered to take her own decisions, the fear still prevails in the subconscious mind. With a smothering relationship with Mohan Jaya has a misguided sense of destiny. She compares herself to Gandhari, "who bandaged her eyes to become blind like her husband, could be called an ideal wife, I was an ideal wife too. I bandaged my eyes tightly" (61).

It is when Mohan leaves her alone and goes off because he was under some investigation for his unethical businesses, Jaya ponders over the agony behind being an unquestioning and dutiful wife and a failed writer. Jaya is compelled to look at the purpose of her life, her existence. She cites the example of Maitreyee, the profound sage Yajnavalkya's wife. Maitreyee is symbolic in her quest for her true identity, her true self. When Yajnavalkya renounced the worldly life and on his way to the forest asked his wife Maitreyee whether she would like to stay back taking care of their worldly possessions. Maitreyee promptly responded that she has nothing to do with something that is destructible. She wanted to know the efficacy of that which is immortality and thus she left with her husband to seek the higher truth, her own self and identity.

Like Maitreyee, Jaya wanted to find herself, seek her space and independence from all the drudgery. She was trying to discover the parameters of patriarchy and the possibilities of resistance. She was now negotiating and questioning her seemingly powerless position with that of a structured patriarchal power. When her identity and individuality is threatened, she decides to break her silence. She stifles under the weight of her own silence which almost destroys her creativity thus shattering her own space and identity. When her own space is threatened, she decides to break her silence by doing what she liked most—writing. She takes recourse in the *Bhagavad Gita* where the final words of Krishna's long sermon to Arjuna [was]: "Do as you desire" *Yathechhasi tatha kuru* (192).

Unlike the Western feminist works, Deshpande does not surrender to an aggressive individualism and a very liberal feminism. Her characters move in a traditional set up but are not tied down by a ritualistic orthodoxy. They search for an identity, they yearn for their freedom, yet they are firmly rooted in their culture. As Adele King writes, they are "aware of the strength a woman can have in a traditional marriage.... This is not the 'power-behind-the throne' often held by European wives, but rather an inner certainty gained from willingly accepting a defined role in society, or perhaps from believing in a religiously determined fate" (1990: 160-61). Similarly, A.N. Dwivedi in his article reads silence as a metaphor of communication between Jaya and her husband; a kind of metacommunication. Though his interpretation of silence is different from the lines of the Western feminism, nevertheless he tries to explore the ethos and essence of Indian concept of women empowerment.

Jaya as a writer frees herself from the colonizing male voice that had transmitted a manipulated vision of her identity, and engages in the process of filling the blank pages of her own story, always silenced and ignored. As a result, the fact of becoming the subject of her own narrations (articulated and structured from her own voice) has given her the strength to chronicle and proclaim her real self. Trinh T Minh-ha, thus, comments: "In trying to tell something, a woman is told, shredding herself into opaque words while her voice dissolves on the walls of silence. Writing is a commitment of language. The web of her gestures, like all modes of writing, denotes a historical solidarity (on the understanding that her story remains inseparable from history)" (246).

By delving deep into her psychic core, she finds that the self she seeks to define is not merely an individual self, but a collective one. The power, the permission, the authority to tell stories about herself and other women comes from her cultural community. This community includes the historical experience of oppression as well as a feminine literary tradition.

The fear of failing held back Jaya from writing. It was not Mohan alone who she had to fight, it was her own fear that she needed to get rid of. She could attain her true independence only when her mind would be free from fear. She confesses, "I hadn't stopped writing because of Mohan; I could not make Mohan the scapegoat for my failures, for I had written even after that confrontation with him—stories that had been rejected, stories that had come back to me, stories that I had hidden here in this house" (145). "...My failures. Of course, Mohan had nothing to do with these. He didn't even know I'd written them" (146).

It was Kamat who recognized the potentialities of Jaya; her fear, her apprehension and her yearning for freedom. He, in a sense, encouraged her to overcome her uncertainties, become more self-aware of her strengths and weaknesses and become more confident in her own unique qualities. Like a pupa who has to undergo a metamorphosis before the final incarnation, Jaya undergoes a "crisis" in which she is forced to address key questions about the purpose of her life, her values, her ideals, her achievements. Jaya deliberately uses the pen name 'Seeta' as an attempt to hide her originality so that her works are published without much controversy and she also escapes possible consequences of falling into the trap of allegedly writing about someone who would resemble Mohan, or his aunt or his mother. It was when Kamat warns her, "beware of this 'women are the victims' theory of yours. It'll drag you down into a soft, squishy bog of self-pity. Take yourself seriously, woman. Don't skulk behind a false name. And work—work if you want others to take you seriously. This scribbling now and then..." (148) won't help her much.

In his book *Writing and Identity,* Roz Ivanic writes that the act of writing is not just about conveying 'content' but also about the representation of self. That is the reason why most people find writing difficult because they do not feel comfortable with the 'me' they are portraying in their writing. Jaya is scared to write her own story—"Self-revelation is a cruel process" she confesses. "The real picture, the real 'you' never emerges" (1).

Through a process of self-reflection and self-definition, partially initiated by Kamat, Jaya ultimately arrives at an integrated, coherent sense of her identity. Pragati Sobti, therefore, mentions: "The novelist tries to establish that is not only the patriarchal set up which is responsible for silencing the women. The responsibility also lies within the victim to refuse, to raise a voice and to break that silence. The novel traces the growth of the protagonist from a state of weakness, feeling of failure to that of relaxation. She accomplishes this through self-assessment and self-criticism."

She reveals her experiences from the point of view of the narrator, from a perspective that comes from closeness and knowledge of the situation. She thus recovers the narrative voice that she had been denied by her male counterparts for the maintenance of the patriarchal structure of the community. She abandons the "margins" of her story to take a central position in the development of her new life, in which she fights to renegotiate her space within her community as well as to re-educate its members into a more tolerant, integrative understanding of life.

Writing is considered a valid procedure of publication of the identity, and it is for this reason that many Indian women writers chronicle stories in which women narrate other women's stories. Deshpande, thus, writes in a genre in which protagonists that are in conflict with the idea of having to show their real selves, choose to transmit it by means of creative devices, a fact that Annie O. Eysturoy defines in the following terms: "The intimate connection between the quest for self-development, a *sine qua non* of the female *Bildungsroman,* and the concept of creativity as a catalyst for self-discovery is the basic theme of many female writers" (1996: 21). Both the writer of the novel and her protagonist adopt the creative process as the most appropriate so as to express the outcome of the search for their identity. It represents a way of liberating oneself and opening up to the rest of the society, and in a defensive way, protecting them behind the shelter of a fictitious character, who vindicates all that they want to fight for.

Louise Sundararajan, a psychologist at the Rochester Psychiatric Center in New York, for example, talks about the therapeutic benefits of expressive writing. She says, "Writing is processing", and suggests that by "spilling out their guts people can be on the road to recovery. Writing is a successful therapy because it addresses both components of mental processing. One component is when you write, you spell things out. You say how much you hate it, or love it, and you use all the feeling words you can think of. But there's another kind of processing, and the two have to go hand in hand. You restructure the whole thing. You take a step back, you look at it, you reflect on the whole thing. That's very important. That's a psychological distance you have to keep. You need to do both", adds Sundararajan in her blog.

By penning her story, Jaya has achieved articulation of her predicament, her constraints, her anguish and has thereby broken her silence. Secondly, the process of reflection during the course of articulation has given her an important insight: she realizes that fragmentation of the self is not possible. Earlier she had cut off the bits of her that had refused to be Mohan's wife; she had denied certain parts of her self. But now she decides to live "whole," retaining all that did not fit in the straitjacket of "wifehood". She had decided not to look for clues in Mohan's face and then give "him the answer I know he wants". This decision fills her with vigour and buoyancy and the novel ends on the affirmative note of hope as against frustration and despair with which it had begun. She concludes: "life has always to be made possible" (193). As Adele King writes, "Deshpande's strength lies in portraying the uncertainties and doubts of women who cannot see themselves as heroic, but who want to make life 'possible'" (1990: 167).

The silence imposed on her kept her from breaking down the barriers that denied herself her own voice, and which forced her to assimilate and perpetuate the colonized depictions of her identity. But as the novel, along with Jaya's renegotiation and valorisation of her identity develops, writing becomes the axis of this (r)evolutionary process.

WORKS CITED

Chakravorty, Gayatri Spivak. "Can the Subaltern Speak?" *Colonial Discourse and Post-Colonial Theory: A Reader.* Ed. Williams, Patric and Laura Chrisman. New York: Columbia University Press, 1994: 66-111.

David, Buckingham. "Introducing Identity." *Youth, Identity, and Digital Media.* Ed. David Buckingham. The John D. and Catherine T. MacArthur Foundation Series on Digital Media and Learning. Cambridge, MA: The MIT Press, 2008: 1-24.

Derrida, Jacques. *Spurs: Nietzsche's Styles.* Chicago: University of Chicago Press, 1978.

Deshpande, Shashi. *That Long Silence.* New Delhi: Penguin, 1989.

Dwivedi, A.N. "Recurring Metaphors in Shashi Deshpande," *The Fiction of Shashi Deshpande,* ed. R.S. Pathak, 1988: 219-20.

Eysturoy, A.O. *Daughters of Self-Creation: The Contemporary Chicana Novel.* Albuquerque: University of New Mexico Press, 1996.

Holmes, Janet and Meredith Marra. "Introduction." *Femininity, Feminism and Gendered Discourse.* Ed. Janet Holmes and Meredith Marra. Newcastle upon Tyne, NE: Cambridge Scholars Publishing, 2010.

King, Adele "Shashi Deshpande: Portraits of an Indian Woman." *The New Indian Novel in English: A Study of the 1980s.* Ed. Viney Kirpal. New Delhi: Allied Publishers, 1990: 159-67.

Sara, Mills. *Discourse.* London: Routledge, 1997.

Sobti, Pragati. "Shashi Deshpande's *That Long Silence.*" *Muse India,* Jan-Feb. 2013.

Sunder Rajan, Rajeshwari. "*The* Feminist Plot and the Natiorialist Allegory: Home and World in Two Indian Women's Novels in English" in *Modern Fiction Studies,* Vol. 39, No. 1, 1993.

6
CHAPTER
Emancipating the Bonded Self: A Study of Shashi Deshpande's *That Long Silence*

Monika Mathur

It may be that we are puppets—puppets controlled by the strings of society. But at least we are puppets with perception, with awareness. And perhaps our awareness is the first step to our liberation.

—Stanley Milgram.

Shashi Deshpande's novel *That Long Silence* (1988) won the Sahitya Akademi award in 1989. The novel emphasises the intention of Deshpande to break the icy "silence" that has surrounded women, their world. The novelist evinces how the silence imposed on women is partly of their own making, and partly levied by the society and tradition. The novel traces Jaya's solitary crusade against the deafening silence that has entrapped the likes of her for generations. Jaya journeys across a plethora of self-doubts, fear, guilt, smothered anger and silence towards her self-emancipation. Due to tradition, religion, society and above all patriarchal authority, women have very limited freedom to control them, yet Deshpande portrays the extent to which her middle-class educated women attain freedom. To Deshpande, the need for freedom for woman does not merely mean the defiance of old-established conventions, it must also make her aware of herself as an individual and refuse to tolerate injustice. Her women do feel the necessity to have the proverbial "room of their own," a place to stand and strive to attain the ideal of freedom and completeness. Deshpande's novels obliquely concretize her conviction that authentic life emerges from self-affirmation that leads to self-ownership.

Jaya's journey towards her emancipation begins the moment when she gets married to a man who is a traditionalist and who has his roots firmly laid in custom. Mohan is steeped in the norms he had learnt in his own family. Jaya has her first and the only outburst with Mohan soon after her marriage and Mohan's response is, "My mother never raised her voice against my father, however badly he behaved to her" (83). Nonetheless, she has to make the first reconciliatory move after days of Mohan's silence. And then she goes silent, keeping her grouses to herself, withdrawn under the shell of silence. Soon their marital life grows shaky and shady. It rests on a thin thread of compromise between them rather than based on love. The cause may be rooted in their choice of a partner. For instance, from the very beginning, Mohan wanted a wife who was well educated and cultured (never a loving one). He made up his mind to get married to Jaya when he saw her speaking English fluently.

The action of the novel is triggered off by the crisis in the life of Mohan and Jaya. Mohan, in his pursuit of prestige and security, had indulged in certain malpractices, as a result of which he now faces an inquiry and may perhaps lose his job. Up to this point, Jaya has turned a blind eye towards her husband's illegal means of earning and corrupt practices. At a later point in her life, Jaya muses, "If Gandhari, who bandaged her eye to become blind like her husband, could be called an ideal wife, I was an ideal wife too. I bandaged my eyes tightly. I did not want to know anything" (61).

Jaya is forced to take stock of her life when Mohan is caught in the jaws of bribery and they shift from their posh Churchgate flat to a small apartment in Dadar, where they had once lived soon after their marriage. Here, the couple sinks into utter silence in a mood of frustration and depression, without talking to each other and without sharing their ideas. Rarely, when he asks questions, she does not find a word to answer them. She states pathetically, "I racked my brains trying to think of an answer" (31). Equivalently, Sarojni and Dandekar, in Kamala Markandaya's *A Silence of Desire* (1960), have led a life of complete inwardness with the brooding silence around them. Silence on the matters of mutual concern gives rise to an unprecedented crisis, which spoils their peaceful domesticity. Jaya, too, is silent even on crucial domestic issues. Veena Sheshadri comments, "One ends up by wondering whether Jaya has imposed the long silence on herself not out of a sense of duty or to emulate the ideal Hindu woman of the ages gone by, but in order to camouflage the streaks of ugliness within her" (Sheshadri 94).

Jaya's review of her relationship with her husband points to an unhappy past. To her, married life becomes unbearable and monotonous, as it moved in a fixed pattern. She states, "Worse than anything else had been the boredom of the unchanging pattern, the unending monotony" (4). Shashi Deshpande uses a beautiful image to describe Jaya's married life, "A pair of bullocks yoked together [...]. A man and a woman married for seventeen years. A couple with two children [...]. But the reality was only this. We were two persons. A man. A woman" (8). Behind this simple description lies the ground swell of frustration in the married life of Jaya, who failed to be closer to her husband mentally.

Jaya is leading a seemingly calm and serene life with Mohan and with two children—Rahul and Rati. But behind this façade, her way of life seems to violate her very nature. For her, the wheel of life moves on small cogs, each well fitted in the groove of a traditional and cultural conception. In her traditional role of a wife, Jaya upholds the maxim that "a husband is like a sheltering tree" (137), and she has hardly ever stepped out of his shadow. Even the imagination of widowhood makes her hair raise, "The thought of living without him had twisted my inside. His death had seemed to me the final catastrophe" (96).

Jaya has arranged her life according to the needs of Mohan's life and his activities. In an unequivocal term, she states that Mohan is "my profession, my career, my means of livelihood" (75). She reduces her wants and desires to the bare minimum.

She, for instance, likes to see advertisements that precede a movie show, for they give her "the illusion of happiness" (4) within the wall of the home. Since her husband does not like them, they start late for the movie. The dilemma of Indu in Shashi Deshpande's *Roots and Shadows* (1983) is a similar one. "I had learnt to reveal to Jayant nothing but what he wanted to see," opines Indu and adds, "I hid my response as if they were bits of garbage" (41).

Up to this point, Jaya accepts a life of passivity for herself. Whatever she practises or whatever she follows is directed by only one consideration—and that is what her husband will think of it. Mohan also expects these things from her. Adjustment and compromise are, no doubt, the signs of maturity but every compromise shatters her individuality into pieces. Jaya is analogous to Tara, in Anita Desai's *Clear Light of Day* (1980), who accepts her loss of identity, and is content to play the role of a diplomat's wife. Equivalently, Nora, in Ibsen's play *A Doll's House* (1879), shows her preparedness to adapt herself in every way to make room for her husband. Nora tells him, "I will do everything I can think of to please you, Torvald [...] I will sing for you, dance for you" (Ibsen 34).

Jaya's psychic war is between the role she has been playing to please Mohan and the person she wishes to be. But this submissive, tolerant and taciturn Jaya is conscious of her own voice. She is conscious that she is "not free. I could feel the burden of his wanting, the burden of his clinging" (29). It becomes a point of challenge for the personalities like Jaya, who finally, resolves to come out of the cocoon when life becomes intolerable for her.

Jaya, in the opening of the novel (when she moves with her man to the Dadar flat), is already in the process of discovering her selfhood. Mohan has always taken her for granted, and this time too he is certain that she would follow him unquestioningly:

> I remember now that he [Mohan] had assumed I would accompany him, had taken for granted my acquiescence in his plans. So had I. Sita followed her husband into exile, Savitri dogging Death to reclaim her husband, Draupadi stoically sharing her husband's travails [...]. (11)

Jaya's sense of defiance can be gauged when she keeps back the keys of Dadar flat, ignoring Mohan's outstretched hand and opens it herself indicating a role reversal and an externalization of her unwillingness, unlike a true *Pativrata,* to concede any authority to him. Jaya confesses that it is only at the Dadar flat (a symbol of her roots and her past) where she finds that she has lapsed into the stereotype of a woman. In her moments of self-analysis and self-scrutiny, Jaya wonders, "how did I get this way? I'm sure I wasn't always like this. [...] When did the process of change begin?" (76). She recollects how she was full of vivacity, intellect and creative upsurge in her childhood. Her nostalgic recollection of her father's words inculcates in her an optimistic approach towards life and herself:

> You are not like the others, Jaya. Appa had said [...] While I, Appa had said, and I had agreed, would get the Chatfield Prize, or the Ellis Prize, go to Oxford after my graduation [...]. You're going to be different from the others, Jaya, Appa had assured me. (136)

Fathers in Deshpande's world display supportiveness towards their daughters and inspire their growth as individuals. Saru's father supported her financially to achieve her goal. The father-daughter equation is excellent in short-stories like "Why a Robin?" and "My Beloved Charioteer." Here, Gita Mehta's Jaya, in *Raj* (1989) and Nayantara Sahgal's Sonali, in *Rich Like Us* (1985) need to be mentioned. Both Jaya and Sonali, though grounded in traditional values, have been trained by their fathers to think aright and independently.

Shashi Deshpande's protagonists are not mere housewives; they are career women too—Saru (in *The Dark Holds No Terrors*) is a Doctor; Urmi (in *The Binding Vine*) is a College Lecturer; Indu (in *Roots and Shadows*) and Madhu (in *Small Remedies*) are journalists. Jaya attempts to carve out a niche for herself in the realm of writing. She is a successful columnist and an aspiring writer of fiction who is "liberal in outlook, sensitive to the core, alive to hurts" (Daruwalla 32). Soon, Jaya has to make a choice between success at work and marital harmony. Although, Mohan takes pride in being the husband of a writer, yet he strongly objects to her themes. Her story about a man who "could not reach out to his wife except through her body" (144), was not only seen as an honest probing into life but also won a prize for its authentic depiction of life. But Mohan's response to the story was most disheartening. He imagines that she is airing their family problems in her writings. Jaya was deeply distressed to know that the writer in her could not come to light because of Mohan, she opines, "To Mohan, I had been no writer, only an exhibitionist" (144). Undoubtedly, this incident had left a deep impression on Jaya's psyche and affected her career as a writer.

In having a writer as the protagonist of her novel, Deshpande depicts the problems that women writers have to confront with. Down the ages, a desire for identity and self-expression has spurred the creative writers. Jaya, instead of expressing her true emotions and ideology, shifts to a convenient style of writing, something that could be published easily. Jaya does not want to annoy Mohan lest that should break her marriage. On Mohan's recommendation, Jaya has then started weekly column "Seeta" which has won the approval of the readers, the editor, and above all of her husband. Here we are reminded of Indu in Shashi Deshpande's *Roots and Shadows* (1983), who too finds her creative writing and self-expression being smothered by her husband. Indu, then, begins to write what her husband and readers want to read and not what she craves to write. Jaya has deliberately annihilated the creative aspect of her personality by ignoring the subject of women's suffering in which her imagination soared high. Thus, Jaya has faithfully practised the traditional role of an 'ideal' wife allowing her talent to "rust [...] in unuse" as Lord Tennyson would express it (Culler 365).

In spite of Mohan's disapproval, Jaya keeps on writing serious stories under an assumed name (as women writers have often done under patriarchy), but now her stories are being rejected. This reversal perplexes Jaya and she expresses her dissatisfaction to Kamat (her upper floor neighbour at Dadar flat) who asks her frankly, "Why didn't you use [...] anger in your story? There's none of it here. There isn't even a personal view, a personal vision" (147). Like Kamat, Naren, in Deshpande's *Roots and Shadows*, is concerned about Indu's writing career and also gives her suggestions about her wrong selection of themes. Here, Kamat makes it clear to Jaya that she has been feeding upon wrong sentimental notions like, "women are the victims," or, that there cannot be "an angry young woman" (147-48). This male-chauvinistic idea about woman's anger is not her own, but has been thrust upon her by the society in general and her husband in particular.

Yet, surrendering tamely is not Jaya's life conception. Jaya is too strong to be content with such devious tactics for long. She has given up this "Seeta" column which means, symbolically, giving up her traditional role-model of a wife. Mohan persuades her to continue writing for the column but now she inwardly refuses to follow his suggestion. Shashi Deshpande hints at the modern woman's refusal to comply with the wishes of the husband.

Shashi Deshpande's women revolt against social taboos, and the cramped, wrinkled traditions and values of their ancestors. Jaya, too, liberates herself from the worn-out social customs and traditions that hinder her growth. In India, a common practice is to give a new name to the girl on the day of her wedding. Ironically, this social practice seeks to supersede or supplant the identity of the woman. Jaya was rechristened as Suhasini by her husband on the wedding day. She has renounced 'Suhasini' for 'Jaya'. This reminds us of Mira, in Shashi Deshpande's novel *The Binding Vine* (1993), who was christened Nirmala at the time of marriage. She too refuses to relinquish her name and identity and proclaims, "I am Mira" (101). But this strong assertion remains a private experience; it never becomes public in her lifespan. Jaya was named by her father 'Jaya' especially to denote victory. In Sanskrit, the term jaya means 'victory'. Jaya was distinct from Suhasini because the latter was the replica of the "soft, smiling, placid, motherly woman" (15-16). On the contrary, Jaya is a self-assertive woman yearning to break out of the yoke. In later stage of her life, Jaya muses, "Stay at home, look after your babies, keep out the rest of the world, and you're safe. That poor idiotic woman Suhasini believed in this. I know better now. I know that safety is always unattainable. You're never safe" (17). Jaya's abandoning the name Suhasini becomes a manifestation of resistance to the stereotyping that is inflicted upon every woman in Indian society.

Jaya is symptomatic of the emerging New Woman. She has expressed her free will by aborting her third child without the knowledge of her husband. She did not consider it necessary even to inform her husband, not out of any sense of fear but because it was concerned with her physical well-being and therefore she has a right to decide. For a feminist, the fundamental right of a woman is "to control her own body and reproductive capacity" (*New Knowledge* 959). Jaya muses, "I'm a free woman [...] I will conceive only when I want to" (63). She seems to join hands with the protagonist in the story "Death of a Child" who asserts, "I cannot imagine that the main purpose of my life is to breed" (Deshpande 44). The protagonist in this story is articulate and committed to her course of action—abortion, despite her husband's stiff opposition to it. Whereas Sita in Anita Desai's *Where Shall We Go This Summer?* lacks Jaya's courage, she is perturbed by the idea of giving birth to a fifth child. Against all sane advice she goes to the island in an advanced stage of pregnancy. She lives in the world of Fantasy thinking that going to the island and to the world of childhood she could prevent the biological process of delivery.

Jaya, a convent educated girl, who was made to feel special by her father in her childhood, fails to find place for herself in the family tree sketched by Ramukaka (her paternal uncle). When she enquires, Ramukaka replies impatiently, "You don't belong to this family! You're married, you're now part of Mohan's family. You have no place here" (143). Jaya's rational mind is baffled by the lack of logic in this argument because the family tree does not contain the names of the women who married into this family. Jaya begins to feel that all the women in the family are just wholly blotted out without any identity or even a name. Jaya strongly protests against this kind of treatment meted out to women in our culture and attempts to give another version of history from women's point of view.

A casual reading of the novel makes one conscious that Shashi Deshpande is not only writing about her female protagonist,

Jaya, who is trying to obliterate a long silence and grapple with the problems of self-revelation and self-assessment but, through Jaya, also about other women, those unhappy victims who never broke their silence. For instance, Mohan's mother meekly endures her husband's atrocities. For years, he has battered her female psyche, but the mother like a dumb animal never resents or questions. Her profession is to look after her husband's comforts, she "cooked rice for him again, for he would not, he made it clear to her, eat, what he called your children's disgusting leavings. He wanted his rice fresh and hot, from a vessel that was untouched" (35). Amazingly, Mohan calls his mother a "tough" woman because her real 'strength' was her 'silence'. Shashi Deshpande's authentic portrayal of the experience of woman brings to mind Jaya's reflections about Mohan's mother, as she states, "I am a woman and I can understand her better" (37). Jaya finds her mother-in-law in an utter hopeless situation where there is no alternative for her, except to yield mutely. She lives colourless life and dies while trying "to get herself aborted" (38). The same silence is observed by Mohan's sister, Vimala, who does not let anyone know about her malady and thus bleeds herself to death.

Shashi Deshpande has tried to articulate the hurts and agonies of women that they experience in a male-dominated society. These women suffered primarily due to their endurance and mute acceptance of their subservient status. It would be naïve to believe that this is a typical Indian malaise. Writers from the West have since long been exploring the corroding effect of objectifying women. Carole Paterman discusses Locke's *Second Treatise,* in which he differentiates between men and women, and concludes that wife's subordination is natural on account of her biology, child rearing and domestic tasks because "women and domestic sphere thus appear inferior to the cultural sphere and male activities, and women are seen as necessarily subordinate to men" (Paterman 110).

The servile attitude of woman is again hinted at, through Kusum's example. Kusum, Jaya's cousin, an unwanted wife, falls a prey to the cruelties of her in-laws, and ultimately finds solace in death. Yet another instance of the sceptre used by the patriarch is the beating administered by a man to his wife in the building in Dadar where Jaya and Mohan have come to live. Jaya hears the sound of blows followed by soft moans of the woman. The man hisses, "Open your mouth, you bitch. Tell me where you went. Speak" (57). There is no answer, and therefore, more blows are inflicted. Another living epitome of the oppressed woman is Jaya's maid-servant, Jeeja. She stoically weathers all that her man chooses to put her through—bouts of violence, alcoholism, adultery or whatever. Jeeja, on the other hand, has no anger, no grievance and no equivocation in her mind because, for her, a woman has no life without *kumkum* on her forehead. Here, we are reminded of Shakutai, a domestic servant, in Deshpande's *The Binding Vine,* whose biggest dream was to have her *mangalsutra* made in gold. Then one day she thinks, "The man himself is so worthless, why should I bother to have this thing made in precious gold?" (110). Shakutai had a hard time with her husband who neither honoured her nor supported her and deserted her to live with another woman.

A woman is harassed with various types of suggestion made by her relations: when she gets married. "Be good to Mohan, Jaya" (138), Dada had advised Jaya, when she was leaving Ambegaon. Ramukaka implies the same in his parting speech to his niece, Jaya, "Remember, Jaya, the happiness of your husband and home depends entirely on you" (138). The principles of complete self-effacement and blind devotion to the husband govern the conduct of traditional minded woman. Again, there is Vanitamami's judicious advice to Jaya, her niece, "if your husband has a mistress or two, ignore it; take up a hobby instead—cats, maybe, or your sister's children" (31). Here we are reminded of the protagonist Geeta, in Rama Mehta's *Inside the Havelli* (1996), whose mother gave her some words of wisdom before the marriage such as to keep her head covered, never to argue with the elders, respect her mother-in-law and do what she would advise and cautioned her not to talk too much in her in-law's house. A critic has rightly called such women "female patriarchs" (Kirpal 102). Such misconceptions have helped men to acquire and command a superior position in society. Jaya often finds fault with the wisdom of her elders, due to which her life has become an endless process of waiting, "Wait until you get married. Wait until your husband comes. Wait until you go to your in-laws' home. Wait until you have kids" (30). These societal compulsions lead Jaya to review her position in society and she realizes that she is an educated woman who has many options in life.

Devoid of her routine in Dadar flat, Jaya turns her gaze inwards and finds that she and Mohan have been skating on thin ice, while the cracks in the floor reveal deep rifts and dangerous whirlpools. Scrutinizing her relationship with her husband, Jaya finds that she is all the time dominated by her chauvinistic husband. Their physical relation always ends up with Mohan's question whether he has hurt her. Jaya does not immediately react to the situation, but wonders, "What if I say 'yes'? What will that do to him? But I knew I would never say it" (98). All this certainly does not show a natural and harmonious relationship between the two when we see that one is unable to express his or her feelings to the other. Jaya's forced relationship and not a natural one reminds us of the protagonist, in the story "My Beloved Charioteer," who states, "When he wanted me, he said, 'Come here.' And I went. And when he finished, if I didn't get out of his bed fast enough, he said, 'You can go.' And I went" (53). Jaya's sexual life gives her no satisfaction for she sleeps "with him, too, without desire" (97). As one of Sartre's characters opines, "it is like drinking oneself without feeling thirsty" (Sartre 52). Mohan's indifference in and after the sexual act often fills her with a sense of loneliness and illusion. She misses companionship, togetherness, tenderness and affection in their conjugal relationship. This situation of Jaya reminds us of Maya's predicament in Anita Desai's *Cry, The Peacock* (1980). Maya's husband is cold, hard and distant. As she pathetically tells, "He did not give another thought to me, to either the soft, willing body or the lonely, wanting mind that waited near his bed" (Desai 9). The damning realization finally dawns upon Jaya that they were merely rehearsing the roles for the future, when they could actually live like husband and wife. Nothing can be more frustrating and depressing than this that they have yet to live as wife and husband even after seventeen years of their marital life.

The modern Indian woman has emerged with different opinion on certain things as compared to her ancestors. The personal happiness, self-satisfaction are the things she wants at any cost, even outside the marriage she can search for it. Jaya, who is unable to cope up with the obdurate husband, automatically gets attracted towards Kamat. This extra-marital affair is the means of assertion for her. Wondered with the joy of this new relation, she confesses:

> [...] it had been a revelation to me that two people, a man and a woman, could talk this way. With this man I had not been a woman. I had been just myself—Jaya. There had been an ease in our relationship I had never known in any other. There had been nothing I could not say to him. And he too [...]. (153)

It is to Kamat that Jaya talks about the most tragic event in her life—the death of her father, who had been so affectionate and encouraging towards her. The memory of that searing experience can still bring tears to her eyes. Suddenly, she involuntarily finds herself in the comforting embrace of Kamat, as she realizes, "there was no more words" and "I was crying and he was holding me" (156). For a split second she is unable to distinguish between him and Appa. Her body responds to his gentle look, voice and touch. She recounts the experience thus, "There had been nothing but an overwhelming urge to respond to him with my body, the equally overwhelming certainty of mind that I could not do so. Later, there had been confusion" (157). But she instantaneously rejects the instinctual urge—it is not in the interest of safeguarding her marital bliss. At home that night, however, she deliberately arouses desire in Mohan and makes fierce love to him in an apparent displacement.

That Long Silence is also a scathing critique of our social institution like marriage, the way it stifles the growth and free expression of the individual. This institution puts the individuals into the slots like wife, husband, brother, sister, daughter, son, etc. and obstructs the free communication between human beings.

Jaya, who belongs to an age of transition and is caught in the vortex of tradition and modernity, cannot enjoy her relationship with Kamat for a long time. Here, we spot dichotomy in Jaya's outlook—modern Jaya does not find anything wrong in her friendship with Kamat, but her traditionally conditioned self withdraws on the question of establishing physical relations. Thus, Jaya is trapped between her freedom to choose and her questioning conscience to conform to rules. Jaya deserts Kamat at the moment when he needed her reassuring presence most—at his death bed. Afraid of the social stigma, she rushes out of the dead Kamat's room and shuts off the thought of her shame and defeat by shutting out the thought of the lonely dead man. Cormack rightly opines, "Girls and women all too often want to have their cake and eat it too. Many want new opportunities, old securities, new freedom, old protection" (Cormack 105). Jaya is also representative of this class. Jaya's refusal to help dying Kamat is her assertion of belonging to Mohan: "I knew it now, Jaya," he had said, and "I had run away. He tried to reach out to me in his loneliness and it had frightened me. I'm Mohan's wife, I had thought, I'm only Mohan's wife, and I had run away" (186). But this is only a temporary escape from an extraneous situation. In her heart of hearts she is aware that by being Mohan's wife she has suffered an irreparable negation of herself—she is never apprehensive of the relationship that ties a woman with a man rather than the man himself, as she mentions, "it was not Mohan but marriage that had made me circumspect" (187).

The soft and cosy shell of matrimony, at last, is shattered when Mohan accuses Jaya of being neutral towards him, specially when he is facing the biggest crisis of his professional life, "I know that I've never mattered to you" (118), he states angrily and adds, "the truth is that you despise me because I've failed" (121). The undesirable and untimely accusation puts Jaya into an aggressive and almost unnatural and insane person. She questions herself, "Then what have I been doing, living with him all these years?" (124). To cap it all, Jaya is horrified that Mohan holds her responsible for his suspension. He squarely absolves himself by declaring that he has been doing it not for himself but only for his wife and children. As he states, "it was for you and the children that I did this. I wanted you to have a good life" (9). A mood of aggressiveness, anger and irritation, overpowers Jaya, but she remains dumb.

When silence fails as a protective cover, hysteria becomes the only shield. The volcanic lava which has been simmering inside her bursts out in a hysterical laughter. "I must not laugh, I must not laugh" (122) she keeps reminding herself, considering the gravity of the situation and fierceness of Mohan's anger, but she does laugh and lands herself in a more hopeless situation. Adesh Pal finds her anger "self-destructive" as she turns the direction of her anger on herself (Pal 122). Angrily, Mohan flounces out of the house and Jaya is altogether broken and bewildered for fear of the social stigma of a discarded wife. Hopelessness and despair thicken with the disappearance of her son Rahul, who had gone with Rupa and Ashok (their friends) on a holiday trip.

The mounting pressure of revolt, which is sapping her energy like a canker in a bud, turns upon herself. Jaya, now, sees herself in relation to her mad cousin, Kusum. "Suddenly it occurs to me—as long as Kusum was there, I had known clearly who I was [...]. I was not Kusum" (24). Without Kusum her sanity seems to be suspected. Is it Jaya herself in another form—frenzied and torn half of herself, battling with the threats to her freedom and her integrity not knowing where to turn to while the clean, compact, conditioned world crumples around here? Does she not have something to call her own which can offer her sanity she desperately needs to save herself from drowning? Sandra Gilbert and Susan Guber opine, "The mad woman in literature by women is not merely a foil to the heroine. She is usually in some sense the author's double an image of her anxiety and rage" (Gilbert 78). The mad woman is usually destroyed in women's fiction, and it happens here also. Kusum's madness leads her to death. Jaya escapes suicide but goes hysteric. Though Jaya's hysterical laughter is a gesture of protest, she has to find the strength to address herself to these challenges if she is to be emancipated and find her true self.

Jaya's disgusted laugher is a 'Cathartic' act for her, less violent but similar to that of Maya, the protagonist in Anita

Desai's *Cry, The Peacock* (1963). Maya's neurosis arises due to the lack of her husband's (Gautam's) concerns. No wonder, her psychological imbalance results in insanity and violence, while that of Jaya ends only in violent giggle. It had been found that "neurosis is caused by bottled up feeling, because when people repress their feelings, they repress their memories and traumatic experience" (Moller 22). Unlike Maya, Jaya soon musters up enough inner strength to stage a return to normalcy.

Outside factors play an important role in Jaya's conformity to family life. Unable to cope up with the situation, Jaya, in an unconscious state, walks aimlessly in the streets and alleys of Bombay, and she is shocked to see two males fondling the breast of a well-to-do girl who is under the effect of some drug, therefore unconscious about her situation. Suresh Chandra opines, "If the emancipation of the woman lies in the exhibitionism of the kind indulged in by the younger set that makes her vulnerable to public molestation, then instead of liberating the woman from the existing tyrannical system it would make her an idiotic slave to man's obscene desire" (Chandra 58). Jaya remains a mute witness to this acquiescing annihilation of the womanhood and prefers to walk away in drenching rain. The impact of the incident is so overpowering on her mind that she, finally, comes back home.

Jaya's neurosis has a sobering effect on her. She makes important discoveries about herself during her neurotic suffering. This idea is strongly developed by Doris Lessing in her *The Four-Gated City* (1969) that the spilt person is a forerunner of a new state in the evolution of man. She opines that through the crack in a person's personality, "the future might pour in a different shape—terrible perhaps or marvellous, but something new" (Lessing, *The Golden Notebook* 405). Like Jaya, Anna in Doris Lessing's *The Golden Notebook* (1962) and Sita in Anita Desai *Where Shall We* Go *This Summer?* (1975) discover new truths about their own nature and their relation with the world and they emerge from insanity to a tentative but fresh state of balance, self-respect and independence.

The novel shows progression as the protagonist undergoes a kind of transformation through self-recognition. Jaya, in the intolerable period of waiting for Mohan and rising hysteria ferrets out her hidden manuscripts—her earlier life, her marriage with Mohan, the frustration and disappointment in her seventeen-year-old marital life, her personal failures, and jotted it down on paper. In this regard, Freud observes:

> As long as things go well with a man, his conscience is lenient and lets the ego do all sorts of things; but when misfortune befalls him, he searches his soul, acknowledges his sinfulness, heightens the demands of his conscience, imposes abstinences on himself and punishes himself with penances. (Freud 318)

But Jaya questions herself, "What have I achieved by this writing?" (191). By penning her story, she has achieved articulation of her predicament, her constraints, her anguish and has thereby broken her silence. Her narrative is what the psychoanalyst calls "a talking cure" (Dinesh 85). Similarly, in Shobha De's *Socialite Evening* (1989) Karuna's tension is also released through the act of writing her own story. For her, it becomes an exercise in introspection and retrospection.

Shashi Deshpande, with her innate pragmatism as well as her middle-class background, does not take rebellion against a male-dominated world to the bitter end. Aware of the fact that breaking off the bonds of family would result in loneliness and disintegration of the larger social set-up, Jaya looks for happiness and self-fulfilment within the family itself. Jaya, after receiving Mohan's "All Well" telegram (189), and after the arrival of the son Rahul, finds herself slipping into the grooves of her marital life again. Shashi Deshpande seems to pose a question to the reader and the society at large: Is it not better for a woman to fit in matrimony with the wheel of independence and carry it along as support, as energizer in the movement of life?

Jaya, finally, resolves to break the icy silence, which has plagued her family since long. It is to the credit of Jaya that she takes the initiative in this matter. Now Jaya's desire is to continue in her married state, with the hope that her husband too would change, if she stopped speaking "Prakrit" (the women in the ancient times were not allowed the use of Sanskrit) and expressed herself as partners in marriage. With new understanding, Jaya opines:

> It's possible, that we may not change even over long periods of time. But we can always hope. Without that, life would be impossible. And if there is anything I know now it is this: life has always to be made possible. (193)

Deshpande has portrayed the feel and tone of Indian life, of ordinary problems in everyday life. A life of complete inwardness, of a subjective indulgence, is not for Jaya. Neither complete conforming nor total draining out of individuality is the proper way out of the dilemma. One cannot live in fragments; the absolute self and the relatedness must join hands and hope for the fuller enjoyment of life.

At this juncture of life, the traditional Indian wisdom stands Jaya in good stead. The words from the *Bhagavad Gita* (the final words of Lord Krishna to Arjuna)—*Yathechhasi tatha kuru* (Do as you desire)—appeal to her after she gains knowledge about her own self (192). This is the situation in which each enlightened soul has to decide for itself the course of desirable action, by following which victory would be courted. This is the state of Jaya (victory). Abraham Maslow believes that the self-actualised person looks inward, and works in order to complete the void to attain individuality in society. He argues, "The self-actualising people are committed to their visions, they use their intelligence; they are realistic about their options and they take risk to achieve their goals" (Maslow 172).

Jaya has also taken a firm decision about her career. She resolves that she is a writer and, therefore, will live as a writer. As Erikson opines, "Even if a woman does not have to work to eat, she can find identity only in work that is of real value to society" (Erikson 208). It is her enlightenment about herself that makes Jaya realize her potentiality to provide something to society. Jaya's service to women is in becoming the angry young writer who attempts to obliterate "that long silence" which has incarcerated women for centuries.

Jaya's realization of her place in the social universe helps her resolve female dilemma too. Jaya viewed her periodical cycle as a curse at the beginning, and now her neighbour, Mukta's daughter, Nilima, also tries to stop her menstrual cycle with the help of pills because she thinks that it is a curse on womanhood and it must be overcome. Similarly, Saru, in *The Dark Holds No Terrors,* seems to be fettered by the natural function of the body. To her, growing into woman is "something shameful" and "torture" (55). Jaya, however, has reached a stage in her life when she no longer considers it a curse but only a means of fulfilment of her femininity. This change in Jaya's outlook is brought about by an objective consideration of obtaining realities offered by Mohan's absence. This development is a stage towards 'Jaya' of the inhibitions within her and without.

Jaya journeys a full circle, from searching her identity in loneliness to her relationship with Mohan and children. But though it is a full circle, it is not the same point to which she returns. Jaya has acquired wisdom in the tribulations of her life. The earlier image in Jaya's consciousness of "two oxen yoked together" automatically stands rejected. Now, she does not wish to relate herself with mythical Sita, Savitri and Gandhari. Instead she prefers Maitrayee, sage Yajnavalkya's wife, who rejected her husband's offer of half of his property and who asked him. "Will this property give me immortality?" (25). This is an example of a character seeking strength from a more vital part of our tradition in order to move towards liberation.

Jaya gives us the new image of the Indian woman who has the prowess to break the age-old silence by refusing to dance to the tune of her husband. To sum up, in Rajeswari's words, "Silence is a symbol of oppression, a characteristic of the subaltern condition. On the contrary, speech signifies self-expression and liberation" (Rajan 83). Hence, Jaya chooses 'speech'.

WORKS CITED

Chandra, Suresh. "Semiotics of Feministic Discourse in *That Long Silence*". *Critical Practice*. III. 1. (Jan. 1996).

Cormack, Margarate L. *She Who Rides a Peacock*. Bombay: Asia Publishing House, 1961.

Culler, A. Dwight. *The Poetry of Tennyson*. New Haven: Yale University Press, 1977.

Daruwalla, Keki N. "An Intense Book"—Rev. of *That Long Silence* by Shashi Deshpande. *Indian Literature*. 34. 6. (Nov.-Dec. 1991).

De, Shobha. *Socialite Evenings*. New Delhi: Penguin Books, 1989.

Desai, Anita. *Clear Light of Day*. New Delhi: Allied Publishers, 1980.

——. *Cry, The Peacock*. New Delhi: Orient Publications, 1980.

——. *Where Shall We Go This Summer*? 1975. New Delhi: Orient, 1982.

Deshpande, Shashi. *That Long Silence*. 1988; New Delhi: Penguin Books, 1989.

——. *Collected Stories*. New Delhi: Penguin Books, 2003.

——. *Roots and Shadows*. Bombay: Orient Longman, 1983.

——. *Small Remedies*. New Delhi: Penguin Books, 2000.

——. *The Binding Vine*. New Delhi: Penguin Books, 1993.

——. *The Dark Holds No Terrors*. New Delhi: Penguin Books, 1980.

Dinesh, Kamini. "*That Long Silence*: The Narrator and the Narrative". *Contemporary Indian Fiction in English*. Ed. Avadhesh K. Singh. New Delhi: Creative Books, 1993.

Erikson, Erik H. *Childhood and Society*. New York: International University Press, 1950.

Freud, Sigmund. *Civilization and its Discontents*. Harmondsworth: Penguin Books, 1985.

Gibert, Sandra and Susan Guber. *The Madwoman in the Attic*. New Haven: Yale University Press, 1979.

Ibsen, Henrik. *A Doll's House*. New York: Dover Publication, 1879.

Kirpal, Viney and Mukta Atrey. *Shashi Deshpande: A Feminist Study of Her Fiction*. New Delhi: D.K. Publishers, 1998.

Lessing, Doris. *The Four Gated City*. 1969. London: Granada Publishing Ltd., 1971.

——. *The Golden Notebook*. 1962. London: Redwood Press Ltd., 1972.

Markandaya, Kamala. *A Silence of Desire*. London: Putnam, 1960.

Maslow, A. *Dominance, Self-Esteem, Self-Actualisation*. Monterey: Brooks, 1973.

Mehta, Gita. *Raj*. New York: Simon & Schuster, 1989.

Mehta, Rama. *Inside the Havelli*. New Delhi: Penguin Books, 1996.

Moller, Alfred H. *Breakthrough in Psychotherapy for All Emotional Problems and Psychosomatic Disorder*. Maidstone: Londinium Press, 1979.

New Knowledge Library Universal Reference Encyclopaedia. London: Bay Books, 1981.

Pal, Adesh. "*That Long Silence:* A Study in Displaced Anger". *The Fiction of Shashi Deshpande*. Ed. R.S. Pathak. New Delhi: Creative Books, 1998.

Paterman, Carole. "Feminist Critiques of the Public Private Dichotomy". *Feminism and Equality*. Ed. Arine Phillips. Oxford: Basil Blackwell, 1987.

Rajan, Rajeswari Sunder. *Real and Imagined Women: Gender, Culture and Post-Colonialism*. London: Routledge, 1993.

Sahgal, Nayantara. *Rich Like Us*. London: Heinemann, 1985.

Sartre, Jean-Paul. *The Age of Reason*. Hamilton: Hamish, 1947.

Sheshadri, Veena. Review of *That Long Silence* by Shashi Deshpande. *Literature Alive*. 2.1 (1988).

7

CHAPTER

Deconstructing, Reconstructing Identities: Shashi Deshpande's *That Long Silence*

Minakshi Lahkar

> The real voyage of discovery consists not in seeking new landscapes but in having new eyes.
>
> —Marcel Proust.

Indian women writers from the late 19th century onwards have often shown the frustration and alienation faced by their female protagonists standing at the crossroads of modernity and tradition. While access to liberal Western education fostered their aspirations for a sense of fullness, wholeness, they found themselves fettered to the conventional domestic and maternal roles within the old social systems. The search for an individual identity has, therefore, involved adjustment between the existential and traditional selves.

In *That Long Silence,* Shashi Deshpande seems to follow a similar route. Her protagonist, Jaya Kulkarni, having spent seventeen years of her married life conforming to the traditional roles, is forced to confront her existential angst—to probe her selfhood and to see whether there is more to her than just being Mohan's wife, Rahul and Rati's mother, Ai's daughter or Dinkar and Ravi's sister. In the words of Anne Collette, it is "the search for a self that casts its own shadow".[1] At the end, despite her self-questionings and her determination to break the mould of silence, she remains bound by the familial order. She thus takes her place in a long row of female protagonists who have chosen to give primacy to their relational selves.

Anjana Sharma speaks of Deshpande's women characters "wrestling with the emergence of their individuated selves, with sexual desire, with the need to have greater control over their own lives, and most significantly, for the need to choose, to a small degree, the kind of lives they would like to live".[2]

Jaya's awakening begins when she and her husband, Mohan, are forced to relocate to a modest flat in Dadar, from their upscale Churchgate home, in the wake of a scam in his office. This shift marks a signal change in their marital relationship. At the very inception, she displays a hitherto absent spirit of assertiveness when, disregarding his hand stretched out for the keys, she unlocks the door to the flat herself.

Despite the initial fright caused by the disruption of the smooth tenor of her life, she begins to experience a "curious sense of freedom".[3] Mohan too, shorn of the comfort of his official routine, is driven to introspection. He had married her as she seemed to fit the ideal of the convent-educated, English-speaking cultured wife he had always aspired to have. He had renamed her Suhasini and she had tried to be true to her role, constructing herself as a "smiling, placid, motherly woman... who lovingly nurtured her family".[4] In reality, she had found family life unendurable, marked mostly by hostility.

She too had seen him solely as a husband and provider, never thinking of him as an individual with his own inner insecurities. Now he bitterly accuses her of selfishness, telling her that she was never a real wife. She is startled by his perspicuity and realizes that they have both been playing out their parts and their marriage has been marked by falsity.

Her meticulously-recorded diaries bear no record of the existential agony she has gone through. Therefore, she must rely on a selective reworking of memory to retrace "the disorderly chaotic sequence of events and non-events" of her life.[5] For Teresa de Lauretis, consciousness is "a particular configuration of subjectivity...produced at the intersection of meaning with experience".[6] It is grounded in personal history as self and identity can be understood only within the particular context.

Though the narrative voice is Jaya's, she makes it clear that it is "our story".[7] Joan Riviere had perceptively noted: "There is no such thing as a single human being pure and simple, unmixed with other human beings...we are members of one another."[8] Jaya's retelling of her life expands to include a whole host of characters who have helped to shape her consciousness.

There is a frequent oscillation between "then" and "now" as she transmutes known information into knowledge. She notes, "I know it now", and the stress on the 'now' indicates how recently acquired the knowledge is.[9] Ghosts of the past, including forgotten aspects of herself, resurface in her mind in the process of her narratological journey of interpreting meaning. Her upstairs neighbour, the long-dead Kamat, is a crucial figure in her burgeoning consciousness. She acknowledges this by saying: "I knew I had to puzzle it out, to put the bits and pieces together and see what form it took, my relationship with this man."[10]

She had established an instant rapport with Kamat who had quickly slipped into the role of confidant and mentor. His ridicule had made her drop the name "Suhasini" and revert to "Jaya," her father Appa's name for her. Appa had kept her within the charmed circle of his love. By making her feel unique he had fostered a sense of separateness, unable to mix easily with girls of her own age. This had in fact been a source of distress in the hostel where she found herself after his death. He had also repressed her taste in music, insisting that only classical music was worth listening to. Appa had been an important influence in her formative years. She had tried, in vain, to publish his story of a young widow, and it had been Kamat who had pointed out the utter futility of her efforts. He had been adamant that she express herself in her writing and not her father's story. Later, after she had achieved some recognition herself as a writer of sorts, she had disdained to be identified with Appa, remembering his failure as a poet. Thus, Kamat had obviously succeeded in helping her grow out of Appa's shadow.

Kamat had advised her to write seriously under her own name. Yet characteristically, suppressing the desperation which once actually made her leave home, she had chosen a middle path—taking up a weekly column as "Seeta". This "had been the means through which I had shut the door firmly for all those other women who had invaded my being screaming for attention".[11] Now, in Dadar, Seeta explodes and she begins to write as Jaya articulating herself as "I" and "me". It is an assertion of her own identity.

Kamat had the sensitivity to understand the seething anger common to all women which found expression in their banging of pots and pans. The truth of his half-jocular statement is borne out to her years later, now in Dadar, when she realizes the anger in Vanitamami, that "clanger of pots and pans"—in having to put up with a domineering mother-in-law and a philandering husband.[12] Later, recovering from her illness, apparently deserted by Mohan, she expresses her own savage anger, clattering the tea things in the sink. In fact, her final acknowledgement of her anger comes together with her declaration that she is no longer afraid. In *Their Eyes Were Watching God,* Zora Neale Hurston had written about anger as necessary weapon against fear. It is, therefore, the memory of Kamat which spurs Jaya's self-actualisation.

At that time, terrified of Mohan's disapproval, Jaya had learnt to control her anger. Yet, critically aware of herself, she had analysed her wifely role as that of a pet dog. Kamat had dismissed her martyr act as an enactment of her "sense of power," categorizing her with all the "bloody looking-after-others, caring-for-others women" who tried to make their menfolk helpless without them.[13] Now, the truth of his assertion comes home to her when she realized that she had been blind to the power wielded by women like her own grandmothers whose children—like Appa and Chandumama—had spent their lives reacting against them. This insight into the image of the repressive mother stands her in good stead at the end of her narrative when she avoids falling into the same trap with Rahul.

Jaya tries to stress the ungendered nature of her friendship with Kamat asserting that with him, "I had not been a woman,

I had just been myself, Jaya".[14] Yet, paradoxically, she also remembers how he had awoken her to an awareness of her repressed eroticism. Her body had sought to respond but her mind had enforced a retreat behind the *lakshman rekha* she had envisaged for herself. Thus, she insists on the primacy of her role as a chaste wife. This same attitude had made her turn away from Kamat's dead body, imagining that she was somehow thereby being loyal to Mohan. Ironically, her relationship with Mohan had become empty thereafter.

Introspection also brings home to her the increasing awareness of being part of a sisterhood of women. Sisterhood, based on a "special female awareness," is an important means of empowerment for women under patriarchal control.[15] Friendship between women can allay loneliness and bring hope. Jaya learns to give up the feeling of superiority and separateness, embodied in her image of herself as a mother sparrow safely cushioned within the home. She begins to acknowledge her kinship with various women not related to her by blood.

She had always despised Kusum as the unwanted childhood double in Ambegaon and later as the madwoman who killed herself. Now, learning to look differently, she is no longer able to dismiss her as the other to her own otherness. Kusum now appears as a victim who has been wronged by all of them. She now sees Kusum's madness as an escape, a way to be "gloriously, unashamedly herself".[16] Alive, she had offered Jaya an easy way of defining herself as "not-Kusum".[17] Now that she is dead, Jaya becomes conscious that she must seek some other answer to the question of identity.

Childless Vanitamami—who had never even been allowed to choose a sari for herself—is "metamorphosed" and now begins to assert herself, so much so that Ai begins to look for a home with one of her children.[18] Even her post-menopausal fertility rituals—earlier ridiculed as absurd, assume an added significance as a flaunting of her wifehood, in the face of Ai's inauspicious widowhood. Jaya remembers that only she had understood her wish to look after Kusum in her illness and she had offered the only words of consolation when Kusum died. Ai had unfeelingly commented that it was for the best. When her younger brother, Ravi, laughs at Vanitamami, Jaya, with her new understanding, is furious realizing that he knows nothing of women.

Mukta—previously cursorily dismissed as "the perfect neighbour," always ready to help, assumes an important role in Jaya's existential awakening.[19] She embodies the bonds of sharing and caring that are so important in black women's fiction. Poor oppressed black women, lacking the prerogatives of maleness and wealth, have always needed to bond together to survive. Patricia Hill Collins writes of "safe spaces" where such women can speak freely and where domination does not exist as a hegemonic ideology.[20] Mukta, her daughter, Neelima, and Manda, the maid Jeeja's granddaughter, create such a space of retreat and healing for Jaya when she is ill and alone, thinking that she has lost both Mohan and her son Rahul. Mukta even takes leave from work to be with Jaya who is touched and shamed into admitting her former superciliousness towards her and others like Kusum.

Mukta loses her reserve and explains the logic behind her choice to go on living with her cantankerous mother-in-law, Mai, even after her husband's death. She had realized that Neelima needed a proper family environment which she alone could not have provided. Thus Deshpande reinforces the importance of the family for the individual. Mukta also takes Jaya to task for her act of betrayal in turning away from Kamat's dead body. She reveals how Kamat's support helped her to find stability as a young widow and how he had poignantly foreseen his own lonely death. Jaya realizes that Kamat is another tie that binds her to Mukta.

Neelima is yet another significant female in Jaya's quest for selfhood. Her recurring visits—breaching "the wall of isolation we had built around ourselves," her probing questions, her perceptive comments and her overt association with crows, which she claims are her favourite birds, all carry forward the mother-sparrow-cow image.[21] In Ai's story, the selfish sparrow cleverly destroys the cow after reluctantly admitting him inside her cosy house. Now Jaya, as the mother sparrow, must admit the crow inside and subject herself to its relentless scrutiny. Yet Neelima respects Jaya's literary skills and tenderly nurses her when she is sick. Jaya is disconcerted by her casually announced plan of suicide, but Mukta is dismissive, confident that Neelima is a survivor who can face the world.

Sisterhood is based on support. So Jaya goes to the hospital to help Jeeja when her initial offer of monetary help is turned down. This marks a change from her earlier habit of assuaging her conscience by simply dropping a coin to a beggar woman. She remembers her betrayal of her first hostel friend—Leena—simply based on her facile condemnation of her relationship with a married man. Her analysis of her friendship with Rupa shows her growing realization that woman-to-woman bonding must be based on an authentic sense of self.[22] She understands that with Rupa, despite years of apparent closeness, she shares a superficial, fragile relationship, merely feigning a warmth she does not really feel.

Despite the growth in her consciousness, Jaya always stops halfway in her protest against the patriarchal and societal norms which enforce conformity. This is a regularly recurring pattern in her life. She is disgusted with her uncle, Ramukaka's family tree where even powerful matriarchs like Ajji, who held the family together, are absent. But she allows herself to be silenced by Mohan when he concurs with Ramukaka. This same pattern of acquiescence in patriarchal norms is played out when she agrees to talk to Asha, Ravi's estranged wife, and persuade her to return to the marital home. Though she has no illusions about Ravi, she does not even think of looking at Asha's point of view. Her perspective of her sister-in-law as a good woman seems as dismissive of her individuality as her earlier nonchalant disregard of Mukta as the perfect neighbour.

Black feminism emphasizes the importance of self-definition as the key to empowerment: "Oppressed people resist by identifying themselves as subjects, by defining their reality, shaping their new identity...telling their story." Black women writers like Toni Morrison portray strong, self-willed heroines unlike Jaya who seems feeble and faltering in comparison, always at the crossroads and never taking a decisive turn to assert her existential self. In Morrison's *Sula,* the protagonist, Sula, has a strong sense of self. She does not conform to the norms of the black community of the Bottom township. Once, chased by a group of white boys, she cuts off the tip of her finger, telling them that if she can do this to herself, she can do anything to them. Out of curiosity, she watches her mother Hannah burn to death, instead of rushing for help. Later, she puts her grandmother, Eva, in an institution, instead of keeping her at home. She has no compunctions about sleeping with the husband of her best friend Nel. This destroys Nel's marriage and also her friendship with Sula. The shocked black community breaks off all ties with Sula but she shows no remorse. Even on her deathbed, reunited with Nel, she insists only on her own unique subjectivity.

In Morrison's *Song of Solomon,* Pilate is ostracized by her immediate black community because of her lack of a navel. Yet she constructs a new self informed by the values central to black survival under oppression. She is able to bond with her nephew Milkman, son of her rich brother whose wealth has deadened his family by cutting them off from black society. She inculcates a strong sense of rootedness in him, based on his African heritage. Her life becomes a testimonial of the woman who "without ever leaving the ground...could fly".[23]

Jaya correctly analyses the antagonistic relations between herself and Mohan and shows great maturity when she refuses to blame him for her predicament and accepts responsibility for herself. However, she remains so emotionally dependent on him that she cannot contemplate life without him. Even in a dream, she is totally disoriented by his absence in spite of the support of a roomful of girls. When he leaves, hurt beyond belief by her laughing at him, she is assailed by a sense of panic and for the first time clubs herself with Kusum in the category of "unwanted wives".[24] She candidly confesses "Without Mohan...I don't know what I am."[25] Rahul's disappearance, while on holiday, is the second blow which sends her reeling with shock. Her identity is determined only by her relational self. Hers is, therefore, the typical "history of the Indian woman's subordination of the existential self to the relational self".[26] Shorn of her domestic and maternal roles, she feels annihilated and this translates into actual physical illness.

Mohan's telegram, cryptically announcing "All well," and Rahul's return providentially confirm her in her relational selfhood.[27] The status of her relationship with Mohan remains ambiguous as she is left wondering whether he is triumphantly signaling a return to their old pattern of life. However, she understands the positive value of learning to see thing from a new perspective. She feels that the reworking of her life has been like putting together a patchwork putting of variegated shapes, sizes and colours. There is no ambitious striving for utopia as she realizes: "I knew that I could never shut out the darkness: the darkness had invaded me.... I knew no life but this one."[28] It is a realization that she shares with Sylvia Plath's heroine, Esther, in *The Bell Jar,* who ends her narration with the understanding that the world does not change and reality has to be faced.

When she accepts Rahul's closeness to his uncle Vasant, she finds that by giving Rahul space to be himself, she is herself finding some release from the constrictions of her own life. She decides that she will speak and actively listen, not simply passively hear what she is told. Listening will enable an authentic response. Jaya, therefore, closes on a note of optimism, determined to be more true to her inner self.

NOTES

1. Anne Collette, "If I Cast No Shadow, I Do Not Exist: The Relationship between Existentialism, Materialism and Feminism in the Novels of Shashi Deshpande," *Desert in Bloom: Contemporary Indian Women's Fiction in English*, ed. Meenakshi Bharat (New Delhi: Pencraft, 2004), 60.
2. Anjana Sharma, "In Exile/At Home: The Urban Middle Class in Shashi Deshpande," Bharat 100.
3. Shashi Deshpande, *That Long Silence* (New Delhi: Penguin Books India, 1989), 25.
4. *Ibid.*, 15.
5. *Ibid.*, 187.

6. Otd. in Patricia Hill Collins, "Defining Black Feminist Thought," *The Woman that I Am—The Literature & Culture of Contemporary Women of Colour,* ed. D. Soyini Madison (New York: St. Martins, 1994).
7. *That Long Silence,* 2.
8. Qtd. in Patricia Waugh, "Modernism, Post-Modernism, Gender: The View From Feminism," *Feminisms,* eds. Sandra Kemp and Judith Squires (New York: OUP, 1997), 210.
9. *That Long Silence,* 80.
10. *Ibid.*, 151.
11. *Ibid.*, 149.
12. *Ibid.*, 145.
13. *Ibid.*, 84.
14. *Ibid.*, 151.
15. Nina Auerbach, *Communities of Women—An Idea in Fiction* (Cambridge: Harvard UP, 1978), 13.
16. *That Long Silence,* 126.
17. *Ibid.*, 24.
18. *Ibid.*, 104.
19. *Ibid.*, 62.
20. Patricia Hill Collins, "Towards a Black Feminist Epistemology", Kemp and Squires, 203.
21. *That Long Silence,* 62.
22. *Ibid.*, 48.
23. Toni Morrison, *Song of Solomon* (New York: Everyman-Knopf, 1977), 362.
24. *That Long Silence,* 125.
25. *Ibid.*, 185.
26. Collette, Bharat 60.
27. *That Long Silence,* 189.
28. *Ibid.*, 182.

8

CHAPTER

Shashi Deshpande's *That Long Silence*: A Critique

Roopali

Transcription of personal experiences in literary world is not new at all. A serious student of English literature while reading fiction must have noticed the presence of the subjective element in Fielding, Dickens, Hardy and D.H. Lawrence etc. in an immense measure. D.H. Lawrence in *Sons and Lovers* has so faithfully transcribed his very personal suppressed feelings so that people in general call it his autobiography.

Shashi Deshpande's *That Long Silence* (1988) has also been labeled an autobiographical novel. Critics and scholars have judged it as the "most technically accomplished novel" (Walsh: p. 117) out of her ten novels. The novel fetched for her Sahitya Akademi Award in 1989. The success of life depends on your relationship with people around you. Sometimes good relations curtail your freedom, eat your time and demand your attention, praise and money. The world of human relationship is very complex, obscure and uncertain. At the level of relationship with in her family Jaya is a failure and hence unhappy over it. At the mental level, Jaya and her husband work at different wave lengths. Mohan admits to his wife about illegal dealings and shady business malpractices along with his unscrupulous chief. Within the home, her son dislikes her and her daughter is indifferent to her. She finds a chasm between herself and her near and dear ones. All is absorbed in a long silence and Jaya seeks and waits for the time to speak. The back cover of the novel *That Long Silence* opens the layers of stress the heroine Jaya is living with: "Differences with her husband, frustrations in their seventeen year old marriage, disappointment in her two teenage children, the claustrophia of her childhood all begin to surface. In her small suburban Bombay flat, Jaya grapples with these and other truths about herself—among them her failure at writing and her fear of anger" (Back Cover of Penguin India, Edition, 1989).

Our analysis and probe in the novel cannot be based on mere conjectures and speculations. Is the novel *That Long Silence* biofic? Biofic is a term which stands for the fictional work based on biography of a well-known personality or author's own life. Recently in Bollywood movies on Milkha Singh, Pogat Sisters of Haryana, cricket legend M.S. Dhoni have come out and they did a good business. For them a new word 'biopic' has been coined. If we delve deep in the biographic details of Shashi Deshpande, we may find a number of similarities with the heroine Jaya of *That Long Silence*. Shashi Deshpande is the daughter of a famous Sanskrit scholar. She did B.A. (Hons) in Economics. Later she acquired the degree of Law. Then, she studied journalism and worked for a reputed magazine. She also did M.A. in English literature later on. Her writing career began in 1970. She began with writing stories and also stories for children. She stayed at Bombay and then shifted to Banglore. If we go into certain other minor details related to Deshpande, we notice topsy-turvy nature of her life.

The essence of every biography or autobiography is its fidelity to human reality. If events related to author's life match with the events of her or his work and correspond to human reality, the work impresses the reader and attracts his attention. The great and famous biographer James Boswell aptly says:

> The value of every story depends on its being true. A story is a picture either of an individual or of human nature in general. If it is false, it is a picture of nothing. (James Boswell in *The Art of Biography in West*, Shukla Sarla, Lucknow Hindi Samiti, p. 61)

In story, biography or autobiography selection of events is very important because every event cannot be included in a life story. About this important aspect, Herbert Spencer rightly avers in the following words:

> A biographer or autobiographer is obliged to omit from his narrative the common place of daily life and to limit himself almost exclusively to salient events, actions and traits. (Herbert Spencer in *The Art of Biography in West*, p. 68)

Shashi Deshpande's *That Long Silence* is not a biography or autobiography, it is a fictional account of an enlightened woman which matches to some extent with the writer's actual life. It is an art to transform the personal into the impersonal or the objective into the universal. Shashi Deshpande has excelled in this art of transformation. *That Long Silence* is the story of every woman. The fictional account of the sufferings of Jaya has been universalized by the art of the novelist in such a way that it becomes the story of every woman of the middle class.

It is not the singular example where critics have caught the reflection of the novelist in her work. In the contemporary Indian English Fiction, Rama Mehta's *Inside the Haveli* (1977) and Anita Desai's *Fire on the Mountain* (1977) are the other two novels which have discovered and portrayed the female consciousness of the enlightened middle-class women who are the protagonists in the above novels. Geeta in *Inside the Haveli* and Nanda Kaul in *Fire on the Mountain* are the two examples of suffocating females who are striving for freedom. But the above two have landed themselves in self-sought bondage and self-sought exile. They have failed in removing the yoke of patriarchal set-up. Moreover, in both the above-stated novels the heroines emerge from the shadow of their creators and they have some resemblances. Jaya in *That Long Silence* gets freedom due to her mental strength and awareness of women's right. But happiness evades her due to the imbalances in relationships. The novel ends with so many nagging questions which readers want to know.

We will certainly do justice with the novel *That Long Silence* if we strip it off from the tag of autobiographical novel. It is very significant to note that some of her novels and stories have been narrated in the first person. Most of the writers have chosen first person narration to provide a feeling of fidelity towards the story. To write about oneself is like a confession which is very difficult to do. In the opening chapter of *That Long Silence,* Shashi Deshpande rightly points out:

> Self-revelation is a cruel process. The real picture, the real 'you' never emerges. Looking for it is as bewildering as trying to know how you really look. Ten different mirrors show you ten different faces. (Shashi Deshpande, *That Long Silence*, p. 1)

The novel's plot completely depends on the hinges of good and bad relationships. The heroine's relations with her husband Mohan and children are far from being happy. This creates a tension in the novel. Some sort of repair helps in releasing the tension towards the end of the novel. Besides the theme of relationship, the theme of urban and rural life and the theme of joint family and nuclear family have also been discussed and portrayed by Shashi Deshpande. Life and topography of Saptagiri has been compared with the life of Bombay. Absence of Appa after his death is badly felt by Jaya. There is a variety of characters who give us a kaleidoscopic view of life. Appa, Ayi, Ajji, Dada, Ramukaka, Chandumama, Makrandmama, Vanitamami, Neelima, Mukta, Kusum, Vimala, Kamat, and lastly Jaya, Mohan, Rahul and Rati. *That Long Silence* is similar to a family soap opera in which several sub-plots emerge and then merge with the main stream of the action.

Shashi Deshpande has portrayed womenfolks with their sufferings, and exploitations at the social and family level at the hands of patriarchal society. In the patriarchal mode of thinking, it is told that male stands for domination and female for subordination. A.K. Bachchan, while discussing female consciousness in Shashi Deshpande's *The Binding Vine,* aptly says:

> The patriarchal theology teaches women to internalize this concept (that they are subordinate) in the process of their socializing. It brings to the fore the concepts of gender which

> are man-made. According to Simone de Beauvoir, the history of humanity is the history of systematic attempts to silence the female. She says, 'one is not born, but rather becomes a woman.' It is civilization as a whole that produces this creature. (A.K. Bachchan, "Female Consciousness in Shashi Deshpande" in *IJES*, Vol. XLVI, 2009, p. 154)

Shashi Deshpande in *That Long Silence* discloses the protagonist Jaya's relations with her husband which have not been very cordial for a pretty long period of their married life. *That Long Silence* is a metaphor for a woman's patience and the action follows when the woman's patience reaches a breaking point. Mohan makes efforts to dominate and to impose his superiority on Jaya. The façade of his superiority falls when first in Lohanagar and next in Bombay he is caught on the wrong side in his job. Mohan fears prosecution. Jaya meets his younger brother Ravi who has political connections with one M.L.A. Dilip. Dilip, the M.L.A., is close to the Chief Minister. As an upright woman, she is a bit hesitant as to how she should handle that matter. Secondly, his younger brother Ravi solicits Jaya's help to bring back his hot-tempered wife, Asha, from her parent's place. Thus, the matter on both the issues remains unresolved. Mohan accuses his wife Jaya in not taking genuine interest in solving his matter. Jaya, who was contributing to a magazine column entitled "Sita", resigns due to Mohan. In addition to this main story there are other subordinate female characters who have their own tales of suffering. One is Kusum. Her condition is so pathetic that her survival becomes difficult. Vanitamami is suffering from cancer. There are other characters such as Nelima, Mukta, Asha, Usha, etc. who represent different shades of female species. There are some odd characters like Kamath. The novel begins when the long silence ends. It justifies the 3rd law of Newton—'Every action has an equal and opposite reaction'.

Jaya's going to a new environment after marriage and her non-compatibility with her husband forms the main stress in the novel *That Long Silence*. Jaya and Mohan fail to adapt to new situations. A good time passes and two children are also born. But no improvement, as far as their relations are concerned, takes place. This situation creates an atmosphere of agony, anguish and conflict. In fact, happiness may stand firm only on the foundation of good human relationship. Vinod K. Singh in an article "Human Relationship in Shashi Deshpande's *Small Remedies*" highlights the significance of human relationship:

> In the novels Deshpande depicts the agony, anguish and conflict of the modern, educated middle class Indian women caught between patriarchy and tradition on the one hand and individuality, self-expression and independence on the other. (*IJES*, Vol. XLVI, 2009, p. 149)

Jaya's inner conflict, her agony and her anguish, awakens the consciousness regarding her place, rights and motives in life. In the situation of swim and sink, she chooses the option of swimming in the troubled water. Though the people who matter most do not change till the end, the novel ends in the hope of a better tomorrow.

Shashi Deshpande has never been a flag-bearer of Feminists Movement. She has a firm belief that as a writer she would portray man and woman without any discrimination. She has repeatedly reaffirmed her firm belief in interview after interview. But she has also added: "I know women better than I know men, so perhaps my books are more about women, and that is about it" (In an interview with Sue Dickman in *The Book Review,* Vol. 19, NOG, April 1995, p. 32—quoted in *IAJES,* Vol. XLVI, 2009).

As a matter of fact, she does not want to be called a feminist writer. She says:

> My writing has been categorized as 'writing about women' or 'feminist' writing. In this process, much in it has been missed. I have been denied the place and dignity of a writer who is dealing with issues centered to all humanity. (Naresh Jain, *Women in Indo-Anglian Fiction: Tradition and Modernity*, Delhi: Manohar Pub., 1998, p. 37)

Shashi Deshpande in an interview with Stanley Carvalho rejects the propaganda literature:

> I hate to write propagandist literature. I think good literature and propaganda do not go together. Any literature written with some view point of proving something rarely turns out

> to be good literature. Literature comes very spontaneously and when I write I am concerned with people. (*Sunday Observer* 11, 1990)

When we return to the text of *That Long Silence*, we observe that human issues related to educated middle-class people occupy a major space in the novels of Shashi Deshpande. Amid human issues, relationship plays a major part in almost every novel. *That Long Silence* has a very wide network of relationships—good and bad, and it forms the basis of the plot.

It we look to the characterization in the novel, we find that characters are either good or bad. However, there are no villains. Human infirmities such as envy, greed, pride, cunningness and haughtiness can be seen in not so good characters. Secondly, we have to judge them from the angle of the heroine Jaya. Appa, Ayi, Ramu Kaka, Dinkar Dada, etc. are good. But Mohan, Ravi, Doctor, Kamath and E.E. etc. are opportunists and may be termed as not good. It is from the angle of Jaya that the story has been narrated. If we evaluate from a neutral angle, some deviations may be found. But Jaya is a metaphor for an educated middle-class woman. Therefore, the judgement must be in accordance with the will and action of the heroine.

The novel's end is unlike many other popular novels. It does not end with the ringing of wedding bells or with the hanging of the heroine or with the tragic death of the hero on the road in loneliness and utter misery. As a matter of fact, there is no ending as such. Life of an individual may come to an end, but time and events keep on going. In the penultimate page of the novel, Ramu Kaka quotes Lord Krishna's message:

> But now I [Ramu Kaka] understand. With this line, after all those millions of words of instruction, Krishna confers humanness on Arjuna: "I have given you knowledge. Now you make the choice. The choice is yours. Do as you desire". (*LS*, p. 192)

Shashi Deshpande ends the novel with the sane advice that humans should learn to change for betterment and life should be made possible. She concludes:

> It is true we don't change overnight. It's possible that we may not change even over long periods of time. But we can always hope. Without that, life would be impossible. And if there is anything I know now it is this: life has always to be made possible. (*LS*, p. 193)

That Long Silence is definitely Shashi Deshpande's masterpiece, cast as it is from the feminist angle.

WORKS CITED

Beauvoir, Simone de. *The Second Sex*. Harmondsworth, Sussex, U.K.: Penguin, 1979.

Das, B.K. Ed. *The Indian Journal of English Studies*. Cuttak: Association for English Studies in India [Vol. XLVI, year 2009].

Deshpande, Shashi. *That Long Silence*. New Delhi: Penguin Books, 1989.

——. "Of Concerns, Of Anxieties", *Women in Indo-Anglian Fiction: Tradition and Modernity*. Ed. Naresh K. Jain, New Delhi: Manohar Publishers, 1998.

Mehta, Rama. *Inside the Haveli*. New Delhi: Penguin Books, 1996.

शुक्ला, सरला. *पाश्चात्य जीवनी कला,* लखनऊ: हिन्दी समिति उत्तर प्रदेश शासन, 1973.

Walsh, William. *Indian Literature in English*. New York: Longman Inc., 1990.

Appendix 'A'

The Dilemma of the Woman Writer

Shashi Deshpande

One of the problems I've had to face as a writer is the isolation one works in when one writes in English in India—an isolation that is emphasised when one is a woman. Writing in English in India, one feels sadly out of the mainstream. For me, the problems amounted to this: there was nothing, nobody I could model myself on. What all the English writing by Indian writers meant to me was this—I could only tell myself, I don't want to write like this, not like this, not like this. One does not often think of this question, but sometimes it looms large and then you ask yourself: Where do I belong?....

The dilemma of the woman writer—that seems too vast, too pretentious a title for these tentative suggestions. What I'm really talking about is: What it means to be a woman writer.

It's ironic that I should use this phrase, for I find the use of the phrase 'woman writer' both intriguing and irritating. I too have thought—when it isn't 'woman singer' and 'woman dancer', why is it 'woman writer'? I have possible answer to that: it's because a woman who writes is put in a separate class. She is not a writer who happens to be a woman. She is, *specifically, a woman writer;* and should be judged as such.

Well, I'm using the phrase myself now, because I'm talking of what it means to be woman and a writer. These are all purely subjective theories—that came out of practice. I mean, like it always is: I started writing first; the thinking about it came much later.

To start off, I wrote exactly what came into my mind. And yet (I saw this much later, not at the moment of writing, nor immediately afterwards) I occasionally found myself slipping into having a male narrator, a sort of male 'I'. I didn't think much of the why's and how's of this, until I got a letter from an editor to whom I'd sent a short story of mine. The editor rejected the story—that's fine, one gets used to that—but the suggestion that irked me was the gratuitous advice given to me by the editor: "Why don't you try this in a woman's magazine?" After the anger died down, I began to wonder: Why did the editor say that? It was a good story. I knew that. I was pretty confident about it. It was not a sentimental, romantic love story either, the kind that would fit smugly into a woman's magazine. Then why was the suggestion made? Is it, I wondered, because a woman's experiences are considered to be of interest only to women? Is it because women's concerns, a woman's way of looking at the world, are considered to have no interest for anyone but women?

And then, for the first time I began to think about the male 'I' in my stories. I remembered what a friend had said to me about such a story. "If I hadn't known that you've written this story, I'd have imagined the writer to be a man." And I remembered how pleased I had been by this statement.

Why did l have the male 'I'? Did I do it to distance myself from the subject? Or had l done that because I, too, had felt that there was something trivial about women's concerns, something very limited about their interests and experiences? Had I been, without my knowledge, so brainwashed that I had begun regarding women's experiences as second-rate? Had I, too, begun thinking that women's writing was sentimental and emotional, and so having a male narrator helped me to pare down the emotions, to intellectualise it? But, the fact was that both the intellect and the emotions were mine. This conclusion inevitably followed this question. Yet the fact remains that I was trying to use an equivalent of the male pseudonym which so many women employed to conceal their identities. In other words, the writer in me was rejecting her femininity. Perhaps I had the idea that to be taken seriously as a writer, I had to get out of my woman's skin. Perhaps, on another level, this was an answer to the question so often posed to me: Why do you write only about women? A question so often asked that I tend to get defensive about it. Then about the critics. It is a curious fact that serious writing by women is invariably regarded as feminist writing. A woman who writes of women's experiences often brings in some aspects of those experiences that have angered her, roused her strong feelings. I don't see why this has to be labelled feminist fiction. A (male) critic said about a novel of mine: 'she can be quite brilliant when she is not raising her banners of protest'. Any woman who writes fiction shows the world as it looks to her protagonist; if the protagonist is a woman, she shows the world as it looks to a woman. This view, I have realized, makes a man quite uncomfortable. But to present this viewpoint is not necessarily to be a feminist. It seems that it is, on the whole, difficult for a woman to be judged purely as a writer. To the critics one is a woman writer. I know literature has to be valued in the social context; but to apply the tag of feminist is one way, I've realized, of dismissing the serious concerns of the novel by labelling them, by calling the work propagandist.

It's like saying that when a man writes of the particular problems a man is facing, he is writing male propaganda. Nobody says that. Why is it said only about women writers?

There is no doubt that some of women's writing is propagandist. Marilyn French's *Women's Room*, for example. The extreme stances taken there—all men are sadists, brutes and all women are victims—are an exaggeration of what is done more subtly in some other novels. In these novels one goes to the other extreme from the romantic 'moonlight and roses' kind of fiction. The author has let anger carry her away. It brings to my mind Virginia Woolf's famous statement about anger getting in the way. This is, I feel, really the woman novelist's dilemma—you are caught between these two extremes—the unreal world of romance, and this exaggerated world of 'shit and beans' (Marilyn French's catch phrase expressing a woman's problems). One way out of it seems to be the one Doris Lessing has chosen—getting away altogether out of this world—she has literally got into space, though this writing seems to me far inferior to her earlier writing which was more woman-oriented. I wonder sometimes whether she has this same feeling—that she was limiting herself by writing about women. There are others like Erica Jong and Lisa Alther who have concealed anger beneath humour. The women in their novels mow their way through their predicaments. It is as if they are saying: "I know I don't expect you to take me seriously."

It seems to me, however, that one has to go through this phase of anger. Even if such writing is tainted, it has its place as leading on to something else. All this kind of writing—feminist, humorous, pornographic—has its place in women's writing, as it has in writing by men. For women, particularly, after so many years of silence, there is bound to be some exaggeration, some extravagance. It's like letting a youngster loose in the world, after years of strict discipline. Women have every right to express themselves in any way they want to. What matters in their writing, as in the writing of men, is sincerity, integrity and professionalism. Women's writing is more tainted, if seems to me, by lack of professionalism than anything else.

What is wrong is that the women who write romances, mysteries, historical fiction and serious fiction are all lumped together as women writers.

Appendix 'B'

The Shorter Fiction of Shashi Deshpande: Search for Self

A.N. Dwivedi

Shashi Deshpande shot into limelight in 1977 with her shorter fiction and has since consolidated her claim to this genre by producing three more volumes—all published by the Writers Workshop, Calcutta. She is not one of those writers who have sported with the short-story form in order to relieve themselves from the *ennui* and boredom of a tense and restive time. She is instead one of those who have taken to this form seriously and with bonafide intentions. She has already earned a number of gold medals, prizes and awards for her creative writings, and her novels are just a detailed exposition of the theme and situation so dear to her heart and so concisely articulated in her shorter fiction.

I

Thematically and technically, Shashi Deshpande's shorter fiction is, in many ways, identical to her larger fiction, and it would be worthwhile to trace a common thread running through both of them. More often than not, Deshpande dwells on desperation and frustration, misunderstanding and incompatibility, sense of guilt and loss of face, loneliness and alienation of a sensitive woman pitted against an ill-mated marriage and hostile circumstances around her. As G.S. Amur remarks, "Woman's struggle, in the context of contemporary Indian society, to find and preserve her identity as wife, mother and, most important of all, as human being is Shashi Deshpande's major concern as a creative writer, and this appears in all her important stories."[1] Deshpande attempts to intimately analyse man-woman relationships within the ambit of family and society, and usually concentrates on the experiences gained in life, recalling yet another instance of Jane Austen with her narrow range and limited knowledge. Like Jane Austen, again, she is primarily concerned with the intriguing problems and the suffocating environs of her female protagonists, who struggle hard in this cruel and callous male-dominated world to discover their true identity as daughter, wife, mother and, above all, as human beings.

II

A search for 'self' necessarily implies an individual's quest for identity in this distracting world. It is a self-analysis and a self probe into the existential problems of a woman. In Deshpande's short stories, the traditional and tabood Indian society provides little scope for the independent growth of a woman. Consequently, she has to undergo a number of restrictions and inhibitions, originating from her terribly controlled life during her childhood, youth, and old age. This kind of attitude is neither reasonable nor appropriate for the fulfilment of womankind; it totally negates the great wisdom and courage displayed by our womenfolk in the illustrious past, forgetting all about Ghosha, Apala, Lopamudra, Gargi, Maitreyi and others. Thus, a search for 'self' is a very valid point of departure for modern Indian women from the shackles of society, for it enables them to throw away the rotten customs and rituals and to instil a sense of dignity and self-respect in their lives. It would be worthwhile to examine how far Shashi Deshpande has thrashed women's problems and situations in a fast-changing social scenario.

When Shashi Deshpande's first volume of short stories, *The Legacy and Other Stories* (1978), appeared, it captured the notice of readers and reviewers alike. K.R. Srinivasa Iyengar considered this work along with Raji Narasimhan's *The Marriage of Bela* (1978) and Juliette Banerjea's *The Boyfriend* (1978), and remarked of them that these writers wrote about "the tears in things, the little upsets in life, the price one has to pay for one's acute self-awareness, and the loneliness that becomes more pronounced as one gets older and older".[2] The 'acute self-awareness', of which Iyengar speaks, constitutes the crux of Deshpande's creative writings. The author adheres to it with utter fidelity and integrity, and it is this that offers an 'existential strain' lo her novels and short stories. It also reveals a deep understanding of human psychology on her part. As a general practice, she evolves the threads of her plot from the restlessness and tension of a married couple. She builds it up step by step until the climax is reached and the realization occurs in the self-seeking woman that in the present social set-up the best course for her is 'to grin and bear', and that human beings are interrelated to and interdependent upon one another.

The first important story in *The Legacy* from the viewpoint of our discussion is "A Liberated Woman", which brings out the temperamental and situational contrasts between a married couple—a successful lady doctor and a frustrated lecturer devoted to his teaching. Owing to their contrastive jobs and situations, they cannot pull on well, and things get out of control when a magazine interviewer humiliates him for his inability to bear the financial burden of the family. He now turns a sadist, torturing her in bed at night in all possible ways and inflicting bruises upon her tender body. The interviewer calls her 'a liberated woman', but in reality she is totally helpless in the given situation. The story-writer comments:

> But what really astonishes me is her feebleness, her attitude of despairing indifference. Surely she, an educated, earning, competent woman, has no right to behave this way...to plug all her escape routes herself and act like a rat in a trap.[3]

As regards the strange behaviour of the husband towards her, he is a suitable case for the psychiatrist to study. In this story, the woman's predicament is similar to that of Sarita in *The Dark Holds No Terrors,* where Manohar behaves in the same abnormal fashion. Sarita feels utterly dispirited and dejected in the face of nocturnal terrors and tortures. In her spousal home, she is no better than "a terrified, trapped animal"[4] and in great desperation runs away to her father for respite and succour.

Similarly, the fatty, old woman portrayed in "The First Lady" finds her life quite boring and meaningless, though she is the wife of a Gandhian with three children and all the comforts of modern life. Even the Independence Day function does not arouse any interest or zeal in her. She blurts out: "Yes, I love my comforts. But for these comforts we've bartered away our immortal souls. And the whole price has not yet been paid."[5] The same sense of boredom and dissatisfaction grips the young married woman in "An Antidote to Boredom". She meets a young widower at her son's school and comes to feel that life can be lived at an intense level in the enjoyable company of that man. She develops, however, a feeling of guilt towards her son, though not towards her careless and indifferent husband. Another story called "Death of a Child" deals with a woman's problem of having unwanted pregnancy and the abortion of the child.

The title-tale in *It Was Dark* (1986) depicts the plight of an unmarried girl having been molested by an unknown young man, resulting in her illegal pregnancy and leading to a great shock. In this tale, the 'man' is identified with 'the dark' or 'the evil', though the girl thinks that both of them are the engines of tyranny and forced submission: "There was no enemy but the dark, no fear but the fear of being alone."[6] Another story in this volume called "My Beloved Charioteer" brings out the estranged relationship between a couple having two little daughters. "The Alien" highlights the predicament of a young, married Indian woman now shifted to England, the land of shopkeepers. Her man is out for most of the time, and she is left to watch her TV and look after her baby. She cannot understand even the type of English the Britishers use. She feels totally lonely and dejected here: "The colour, she thought bleakly of hopelessness and despair. Even a fog would be better than this nothingness."[7] Through the images of 'bleak colour' and 'fog', the woman's great disquietude, alienation and frustration are beautifully suggested in this story.

The third volume of Deshpande's stories. *It Was the Nightingale* (1986), portrays man-woman relationship on a different footing altogether. The separation of the wife, Jaya, from her husband for two years is borne with love and optimism. In "A Man and a Woman" a woman comes into physical contact with a boy of seventeen after her husband has been long dead. The boy is actually the younger brother of her dead husband, Jayanta. She is thirty years old, and yet she is full of beaming beauty and youth. Nature seems to have created her for "the joy of life, a body made for a man's hands".[8] For quite some time, she has been overwhelmed by the questions of morality, conventionality and social taboos, but now she becomes very restless and uneasy. Her family rebukes her for buying "a red and blue sari"[9] even after becoming a widow. But for her loving son, Ramesh, she would have killed herself. She is beset with existential problems. She is a mere B.A. and will not be able to secure a suitable job. Then, where should she go?

> Where to? Where shall I go, Manu? My parents are dead. My brothers...no, I can't live with them. And I have become incapable of living by myself.[10]

A similar question was raised by Sita in Anita Desai's novel *Where Shall We Go This Summer?* (1975), when she got completely bored and disgusted with her Bombay life and its sickening surroundings. The answer to this question is to be found within oneself, not in external sources. Didn't Socrates say, 'Trust thyself?' The *Gita* also exhorts not to 'conduct oneself against one's own self'. If one transgresses one's self, one will experience "a living death" (39), as Lalita of Deshpande's story does. The story becomes suggestive enough when it forwards the idea that an effective 'antidote' to the life of boredom, joylessness and alienation is the re-marriage of a young widow. It is thoughtfully executed. Manu, the crippled classmate and bosom friend of Jayanta, comes forward with his proposal to marry Lalita, whose initial resistance to his proposal is nothing but the dread of a tabooed society and false sense of prestige for the members of Jayanta's family.

Anther story in this volume entitled "The Window" has a lesbian touch about it. The bulky landlady whose husband is no more alive, living all alone in her two-storeyed building, lets out two rooms to a newly married couple, and when the man goes out to teach in a school, she opens the window with a fierce jerk and jumps into the young woman's room and pesters her with all sorts of odd questions. While going out of the room, the landlady blurts out: "You're pretty. Very pretty. Does he ever tell you that?" (50). She invites her upstairs, and the young woman starts crying aloud. A different kind of love-affair—romantic, filmy, villainous and gruesome—is portrayed in "Anatomy of a Murder", where a young slum-dweller working as an assistant in a grocery shop and being very fond of movies, catches a glimpse of a white-skinned, well-educated, and middle-aged woman and instantly becomes infatuated with her. He misinterprets her smiles and takes a bag of provisions to her flat, and on being asked to close the door after him pounces upon her in a sudden spurt of emotions and throttles her then and there. Then he sits beside her "still and motionless" (58), without committing any act of robbery or rape. The story definitely demonstrates the disastrous impact of romantic and melodramatic movies on young minds.

The fourth and till date the last volume of Deshpande's short stories opens with "The Miracle". It is more concerned with the miracle of worshipping a monkey called Raaja (who does not die even after getting a dose of poison by a research-prone doctor) than with the question of self-searching. But we discover a fairly good deal of self-searching in "I Want...", where a twenty-seven-year-old woman named Alka is subjected to "the insolent stares, [and] the impertinent questions"[11] by the groom's party. The young woman feels much uneasiness, consternation, and hopelessness. She ruminates: "The woman in me was outraged and protested. I crushed her. She had no place there. None at all."[12] She is terribly stirred within and remarks: "Sometimes I feel we are all doomed to be strangers to one another, forever sealed in separate glass jars we call 'self'" (36). What keeps Alka apart from the common women is a strong sense of 'self' that she wants to preserve at all costs. In a mood of self-preservation, she observes: "I had a shape and form I had to preserve. A self I had to treasure" (37). Clearly, she is a woman of consciousness and wants to discover her integral identity. As regards marriage, she has little or no choice of her own; her parents are there to safeguard her interests. But Alka, being a thinking woman, has her own desires to fulfil. Though she does not want a husband having a four-figure salary or a car, she still desires a man who "hears my voice when I speak. Who understands me even when I don't..." (42). In the end, she accepts the reassurances of her Baba. Another story "Madhu" narrates the wayward ways of a young girl of that name, driving her mother to fury and irritation and her father to the hospital with a severe heart-stroke. Her brother, Vinay, is away in Bombay doing his medical course. Towards the close of the story, Madhu realises that 'sacrifice' is a noble virtue in human beings, and in a mood of remorse remarks: "I'll sacrifice something I like very much and maybe I'll get the other thing" (53). This is, of course, a vague realisation on her part, and a belated one too. But 'All's well that ends well'.

III

The search for 'self' is a recurrent theme in Shashi Deshpande's short storjes and novels. One may keep her stories and novels side by side in order to realise their close concord in respect of subject-matter and treatment. In reality, one is an extension of the other in this regard. As we have seen in the stories, Deshpande's women are usually sensitive and thoughtful creatures, who ruminate over their fate and position in a conservative society. They endeavor to know what they are, how menfolk behave with them, why they slump into inanity and desperation, and why they feel alienated and truncated. Evidently, Deshpande is at home in portraying her women characters in dismal and dreadful conditions. In this matter she reminds us of the disquietude, frustration and helplessness of the female protagonists in Anita Desai's novels.

The search for 'self' is so insistent in Deshpande's fictional world that one does not feel a change of thought or climate anywhere. Her first novel, *The Dark Holds No Terrors* (1980), for example, depicts Sarita as a person divided into two halves—a "two in one woman" who is hardly better than "a terrified trapped animal".[13] As a willful child, she marries Manohar out of her caste and against the wishes of her parents. But after a few years of happy married life they drift apart mentally and emotionally. The plight of totally terror-stricken, helpless and exhausted Sarita is beautifully brought out in the following passage:

> The dream, the nightmare, whatever it was, continued. Changing now, like some protean monster, into the horror of rape. This was not to be death by strangulation; it was a monstrous invasion of my body. I tried to move, twisting my body, wriggling under the weight that pinned it down. It was impossible. I was pinioned to a position of an abject surrender of my self. I began, in sheer helplessness, to make small whimpering sounds, piteous cries.[14]

Getting no respite from her nocturnal tortures and terrors, Sarita goes away to her lonely father leaving behind her two children and husband, only to return at the close of the novel, like Sita of Anita Desai's *Where Shall We Go This Summer*?

Similar is the predicament of Jaya of *That Long Silence* (1988), who is presented as a torn 'self' between what she was before marriage and what she is after it. Adele King characterises these unfortunate developments as "odd misfits", "petty bickerings over money" and "jealousy over affections".[15] The couple develop an icy relationship and observe an unbreakable 'long silence'. In a fit of anger Jaya calls Mohan's mother a 'cook' (which she surely was). Mohan never expected this from his well-educated and well-cultured English-speaking wife. He has always thought that anger makes "a woman unwomanly".[16] His dreams are now shattered, and he slumps into a long-drawn silence. Jaya starts wondering whether "there is such a thing as oneself, intact and whole, waiting to be discovered".[17] She is a victim of circumstances, of "an atmosphere of apathy and boredom".[18] Hers is an alienated 'self' by all means, longing for love and companionship.

Shashi Deshpande's relentless search for 'self' in her short stories as well as in her novels shows that she has largely confined herself to the problems and tortures of the female world. Nowhere does she encourage her female protagonists to rise in rebellion against the males in family matters; instead, she wants to build a harmonious relationship between man and woman in a spirit of give-and-take, in a mood of compromise and reconciliation. She maintains that that man and woman are like the two wheels of a chariot, and that no chariot can race forward if either of the wheels goes out of order. A proper co-ordination, a reasonable mutual understanding between husband and wife is essential for a happy married life. This is the clear-cut message of Shashi Deshpande.

NOTES

1. G.S. Amur, "Preface" to Shashi Deshpande, *The Legacy & Other Stories*. Calcutta: Writers Workshop, 1978, 10.
2. K.R. Srinivasa Iyengar, "Postscript", *Indian Writing in English*. New Delhi: Sterling, 1984, 761.
3. Deshpande, *The Legacy,* 29.
4. Shashi Deshpande, *The Dark Holds No Terrors*. New Delhi: Penguin India, 1990, 134, 215.
5. *The Legacy,* 35.
6. Shashi Deshpande, *It Was Dark*. Calcutta: Writers Workshop, 1986, 23.
7. *Ibid.,* 55.
8. Shashi Deshpande, *It Was The Nightingale*. Calcutta: Writers Workshop, 1986, 32.
9. *Ibid.,* 37.
10. *Ibid.,* 38.
11. Shashi Deshpande, *The Miracle*. Calcutta: Writers Workshop, 1986, 36.
12. *Ibid.,* 37.
13. Deshpande, *The Dark Holds No Terrors,* 134.
14. *Ibid.,* 11-12.
15. Adele King, "Shashi Deshpande: Portraits of an Indian Woman", in *The New Indian Novel in English,* ed. Viney Kirpal. Delhi: Allied Publishers, 1990, 165-66.
16. Shashi Deshpande, *That Long Silence*. New Delhi: Penguin India, 1989, 83.
17. *Ibid.,* 69.
18. Madhu Singh, "Intimate and Soul-Searching Portrayals of Marriage", *Indian Book Chronicle* (July 1993), 22.

Appendix 'C'

Recurring Metaphors in Shashi Deshpande's Novels

A.N. Dwivedi

Through analogies, similes and metaphors, an author renders his expressions concise, concrete and condensed. Of all the literary devices employed by an author metaphors speak volumes of his or her mental attitude and concentration of vision. That is why Aristotle allotted the pride of place to metaphor in an artistic creation. He remarked:

> But the greatest thing by far is to be a master of metaphor. It is the one thing that cannot be learnt from others; and it is also a sign of genius....[1]

Obviously, a metaphor is very helpful in image-making, in concretising emotions, and in crystallising moods. As C. Day Lewis maintains: "An epithet, a metaphor, a simile may create an image...."[2] A metaphor is, thus, a recognized literary device to capture the intensity of an artist's creative vision and the fertility of his imagination. In a brilliant essay, Middleton Murry attributes the qualities of 'intensity' and 'fertility' in artistic matters to 'the non-measurable world' created with the help of metaphors:

> All metaphor and simile can be described as the analogy by which the human mind explores the universe of quality and charts the non-measurable world.[3]

In other words, metaphor is closely related to 'the universe of quality' in artistic creations.

This appendix endeavours to explore some of the recurring metaphors in the fictional works of Shashi Deshpande. These metaphors include 'the dark' and 'the sunlight', 'death' and 'life', 'silence' and 'the binding vine'. They tend to neatly summarize the fluctuating moods and the mysterious emotions of a sensitive woman. Though these metaphors are not too many in number, they put on the track the running wheel of her fictional world. They clearly reveal the inner workings of the protagonists' minds and the emotional ripples in their hearts.

II

The very first novel, *The Dark Holds No Terrors* (1980), is built around the metaphor of 'the dark' and 'the light'. There was a time when Sarita (or Saru), the protagonist, was afraid of 'the dark' at night fearing that a man would invade her body and commit monstrosities upon her. The woman, who had been so defiant in her childhood and adulthood,[4] felt utterly helpless and panic-stricken with the approach of the terrible dark. She described her none-too-happy condition in the following manner:

> Panic and terror mounted in me as the hands, deliberately, with a kind of casual cruelty, gradually tightened round my throat. Oh God, I was going to die.[5]

The suffocating dark, the heavy weight, the pain and the hurt associated with the sexual act made her life a hell, and she longed to see the light, to have relaxation, and to emerge out of a sickening state of *ennui,* boredom and exhaustion. In this novel, the metaphor of 'the dark' is inseparably linked with "panic and sensation" simultaneously (12).

As the novel opens, Sarita is already in the grip of "the familiar irritation, the familiar exasperation" (17) owing to an unbridgeable gulf between herself and her husband even after their companionship of fifteen long years. She is a medical doctor by profession and self-reliant woman by all means; yet her marriage with Manohar (or Manu) has not proceeded smoothly. So, she turns back to her parental home, leaving behind her children. She is seized with a "strange new fear of disintegration" and a "terrified consciousness of not existing" (22). The real cause of the disintegration of the family is a searching interview of Manohar by a lady reporter for a women's magazine: "How does it feel when your wife earns not only the butter but bread as well?" (35-36). Since then, Manohar becomes a sadist, torturing Saru in bed at night. Her dreams of a happy home with children twittering about and a loving husband to prop her up in the struggle of life are now totally shattered. She wants to "sleep peacefully the night through. To wake up without pain. To go through tomorrow without apprehension" (27), but she does not find the congenial atmosphere of her parental house and its peaceful surroundings.

Saru's parental home is in contrast to her spousal home, where, in her own words, "Terror waited for me in our room. I could not escape it" (79). Her desire to disclose the tortures and terrors of the night to Manu evaporates into thin air with the appearance of the sun on the eastern horizon. But when Manu goes on repeating his actions at night, Saru goes away, leaving behind her family and associations and also aches and bruises and apprehensions. To her father she confesses her tortures and terrors caused by Manu, reducing her to a "two-in-one woman" and a "terrified, trapped animal" (134). She has certainly suffered unspeakably and at times she thinks that her sufferings are a return of her own misdeeds in the past of the drowning of Dhruva in a deep pond in early childhood, of the miserable death of her disgruntled mother, and of her improper conduct as a housewife (deriving undue favours from an ambitious man like Boozie). Her terror persists with her like a canker: "When the light comes on, it goes away. When the dark comes, it returns" (205). At moments she feels like "a trapped animal" (215) full of desperation, loneliness and failure. The 'dark' engulfs her completely, and she yearns for the 'light'. In *The Dark Holds No Terrors,* 'the dark' and 'the light' are frequently used as the contrastive metaphors. While the former denotes fear and sorrow, dejection and estrangement, the latter signals joy and fearlessness, company and compassion.

The metaphor of 'the dark', with the same signification, is also used in one of the short stories of Shashi Deshpande. The story "It Was Dark" brings out the miserable lot of an unmarried girl having been molested by an unknown young man, resulting in an unspeakable shock to her owing to an illegal pregnancy.

In the story the man is identified with 'the dark' or with 'the evil'. The unfortunate girl of the story eventually veers round the idea that the 'dark' represents the engines of tyranny and forced submission: "There was no enemy by the dark, no fear but the fear of being alone."[6] The metaphor of 'the dark' is here associated with fearfulness and tyranny.

Another dominant metaphor operating in Shashi Deshpande's fiction is 'death', which remains in sheer contradiction to 'life'. In two of her earlier novels—*If I Die Today* (1982) and *Come Up and Be Dead* (1983)—this metaphor comes out clearly, though in later novels, too, the idea of 'death' is not altogether absent. In *If I Die Today* and *Come Up and Be Dead,* the metaphor of 'death' becomes powerfully evocative and assertive.

As *If I Die Today* begins, we are introduced to Guru coming from his village to get admitted to a modern medical college and hospital set up by Sethji for the treatment of cancer. A disappointed Meera states the following about the pitiable condition of Guru:

> ...Ashoka tells me there's no hope for him at all. He's going to die. I mean, they're going to operate on him,.... He'll die in any case.[7]

Though others are scared of Guru's impending death, he himself is not. Philosophically he remarks: "If I die today, you die tomorrow" (7). Clearly, Guru has "risen above all human weaknesses and crossed that dreadful barrier...the eternal human fear of death" (9). According to Manju, Guru is a detached 'spectator', and Meera also thinks of him in the same way. Manju and her husband Vijay, however, live in a world of make-beliefs and speculations. Manju even laughs at Guru's matter-of-fact approach to life. The Dean, his sister Dr. Vidya Agarwal, and Dr. Kulkarni seem to be very serious about their medical profession. Dr. Vidya is an abnormal woman—a case fit for the psychiatrist. She leads a secluded life with her brother, while her sister-in-law, Rani, lives far away in a flat in Bombay. Rani joins the Dean only when her two children return home from the boarding schools. Dr. Vidya's occasional derangements are so fierce that she first kills Guru, then Tony, and finally makes an unsuccessful bid on Vijay. She appears to be always disarrayed and jittery, always fear-ridden and shame-faced. At the dinner hosted by Rani, Guru and Manju speak of a convict who has slain "more than forty people" (27). The medical campus is also agog with deaths and murders, including that of a labour leader Prabhakaran Tambe. Thereafter, Guru dies "in his sleep" (53), and it is whispered around that he was murdered by one of the medical staff. Then the death of Sumanta's wife is reported, and an erstwhile nurse Vimala is implicated in it. Tony is also killed for his quarrelsome outspokenness. As sensitive Mriga, Dr. Kulkarni's daughter, informs: "Tony uncle...he's dead. He's floating in the tank near the temple" (88). This very girl once dreams of her imaginary accident and her admission to a hospital where her rude father would come rushing, and then she would console him: "'Don't cry, daddy'. And then I would die with a smile on my face and he would be heart-broken for ever after" (91). The girl wishes that her parents were dead, particularly her hard-hearted father. Towards the close of the novel, Dr. Vidya, behaving like an "insane animal" (133), in one of her fits makes a murderous assault on Vijay in the dark of night. The metaphor of 'death', as stated earlier, works as a contrast to that of 'life', about which the narrator remarks: "Every human being has the right to live out his full span of life" (137).

The metaphor of 'death' is emphatically employed in *Come Up and Be Dead* (1983). The novel opens with the premature death of Mridula Dutta of the 10th standard. Some think that she died of "brief illness"[8] caused by a terminated pregnancy, while others believe that it was a case of suicide (23). Though the novel briefly mentions the "peaceful, tranquil death" (98) of Devayani's (or Devi's) father, it is largely preoccupied with the mysterious death of Mridula. First, they suspect Pratap, the nutty brother of the school Head Mistress working as a peon-gardener there, to be the cause of her sad death, and the Head Mistress is also implicated in the case. In the midst of rumours afloat, Pratap is called out of his room and killed in cold-blood. According to the narrator Devi, "Pratap's death had been no accident. He had not died because of a fall from a ladder. Someone had killed him" (144-45). Thereafter, Mrs.

Jyoti Raman, the weak-eyed and spectre-thin mother of Sonali (or Sona) is "strangulated with her own scarf" (172) on the occasion of the Annual Festival. Last of all, the seventeen-year-old Sharmila is stabbed by her own lover, Sanjay. The last few pages of the novel inform us that Dr. Girish, who is ever in need of ample money for his demanding, smart and spendthrift wife, and Mr. Varma, who is "a sorrowful widower" (264), are the real villains of the piece. Of the two, Mr. Varma is worse for having run a call-girl racket at the hotel Open Sesame.

The two novels *If I Die Today* and *Come Up and Be Dead* contain a lot of thrill and suspense in them, and they clearly betray Shashi Deshpande's readings in Agatha Christie and Sherlock Holmes. The same sort of atmosphere also pervades *The Binding Vine* (1993). The narrator, a clever and sharp-tongued woman called Urmi (or Urmila), is seen grieving over the untimely death of her young daughter Anu. Her sailor-husband lives far off, and is a rude and rough person. The narrator does not want to die in any situation; instead, she says, "...I would feel life tingling through me. I was alive, I could not be dead, I would never know what it felt like to be dead."[9] Urmi busies herself for a while in the poetry of her long-dead mother-in-law, Mira, whose poetry, like her life, was full of pity, rage and anguish (67). Mira bled to death after her child, Kishore (Urmi's husband), was born (136). The heart-rending story of Mira runs parallel to the equally, or even more, disgusting story of Kalpana, a young and beautiful girl hanging between life and death, scuttling between home and hospital. Kalpana is also a victim of rape and torture, and her helpless mother, Shakuntala (or Shakutai), is terribly upset and shocked over the cruel incident. Commenting on the deteriorating condition of Kalpana, the narrator says:

> ...I notice how the contours of her face have changed, the bones pushing themselves against the parchment-like skin. There is a kind of deathly stillness about the body, the face almost a mask in its rigidity. (109)

Shakutai wants her own death as well as that of her daughter (177). The title of the novel, in fact, comes from the last poem of Mira's on the theme of love. The 'binding vines' for Urmi are her son Kartik and her mother Inni; for Akka it is Bhaskar; for Shakutai, her daughter Sandhya and her sister Sulu; and for Vanaa, her man Harish. In the course of the story, however, Shakutai's kind and loving sister ends up her life by setting herself aflame after sprinkling "a whole bottle of kerosene" (188). Somehow Sulu comes to know that her own husband has wrecked the life of Kalpana to satiate his wolfish desires, and she is left with no option but to commit suicide. However, the novel ends on an optimistic note, and in the midst of deaths, rapes, and tortures, the narrator is seen searching for "the spring of life" (203).

The metaphor of 'death' is also operative, though on a much smaller scale, in Shashi Deshpande's short story entitled "Death of a Child". This story deals with the problem of a woman's unwanted pregnancy and her subsequent decision to get it terminated. The woman is always obsessed with the question of her own survival: "I don't want it. I can't."[10] She heaves a sigh of relief when the child is finished, and yet remarks: "I feel as we walk away, that I am not alone. I feel that the ghost of my dead child walks with me."[11]

In Shashi Deshpande's novels 'silence' recurs insistently. Saru says in *The Dark Holds No Terrors:* "Silence had been a habit for us" (199); Indu in *Roots and Shadows* (1983) says about her cold relationship with Jayanta that "I am passive. And unresponsive. I'm still and dead;"[12] and in *The Binding Vine,* Urmi adopts a posture of 'silence' on being asked by Bhaskar, her lover, about her none-too-happy marriage with Kishore. "I can say nothing. The silence stretches between us" (161). But it is in the Sahitya Akademi Award winning novel *That Long Silence* (1988) that the metaphor of silence is worked out majestically. In this work, the narrator-heroine's dreams of having a happy home with her husband Mohan and children prove to be a chimera at long last. The corrupt practices of her husband in his office and his overgrowing jealousy towards her literary career create a wide chasm between them, and they adopt an unbreakable yet unnerving silence towards each other. As elsewhere, here too 'silence' denotes lack of communication, frigidity of feeling, and want of understanding and compassion.

Being devoid of emotions in real life, Jaya's short stories become emotionless and puerile. As Sarabjit K. Sandhu remarks,

> This unhappiness is reflected not only in the [Jaya's] conjugal life, but also in social life. Her books, her stories lack anger and emotion.[13]

The result is that Jaya loses her "personal vision",[14] her individuality, and her identifiable features, and that she miserably fails in her writings. A strained relationship with her husband creates a void in her married life, which ultimately results in failure and frustration in her creative activity. There is a complete communication-gap between the couple, and they drift apart. Jaya finds a good companion for herself in her neighbour Kamat, and she discusses with him her personal problems in an uninhibited way. In due course, they become so intimate with, and fond of, each other that they start making physical advances. After his sudden death, Jaya continues to live with Mohan but in a mood of "emptiness" (185). When the mood of loneliness and truncation overpowers her, she realises the mistake of leading a marooned and cocooned life, and finally resolves to "erase the silence" between herself and Mohan (192). Her resolve to speak to her husband and to listen to him intently cuts the ice. Both Jaya and Mohan realise that they are complementary to each other in real life. They begin to speak the human tongue and express human emotions, and thus usher in a new kind of life based on understanding and harmony. To the relief of readers, the wall of 'silence' is broken asunder at the close of the novel.

III

All the novels examined above combinedly enforce the idea that the novelist has all along been striving towards self-discovery or quest for identity. In them she makes a powerful study of female psyche and its problems. She unmistakably highlights women's helpless and hapless situation, their existential dilemma, their want of understanding or compatibility with their husbands. Even a cursory glance at her novels like *The Dark Holds No Terrors* and *That Long Silence* corroborates it. In *The Dark Holds No Terrors,* Saru is riven between two selves; in other words, she is a "two-in-one woman" and "a terrified trapped animal" (134). She marries an educated boy out of her caste and against the wishes of her parents, but after a few years of happy married life she feels suffocated and estranged from him and drifts apart. Saru is a successful doctor and earns the bread and butter for her family, while her husband is a poor college teacher depending largely upon his wife in financial matters. An unexpected interview by a lady reporter for a woman's magazine turns Manu a 'sadist', who adopts all sorts of tricks to torture his wife at night. As a result, she becomes totally terror-stricken and tension-ridden. Her helplessness in the given situation is pathetic:

> The dream, the nightmare, whatever it was, continued. Changing now, like some protean monster, into the horror of rape. This was not to be death by strangulation; it was a monstrous invasion of my body, wriggling under the weight that pinned it down. It was impossible. I was pinioned to a position of an abject surrender of my self. I began, in sheer helplessness, to make small whimpering sounds, piteous cries. (11-12)

Getting no respite from her nocturnal tortures and terrors, Saru decides to leave for her parental house, leaving behind her two children and husband, only to return at the end of the novel. The message seems to be that a married woman has no other place to live and be happy than her husband's. No proper remedy is offered to Saru's terrors and tortures, to her emotional and mental hurts. Her pitiable conditions remind us of those of Sita in Anita Desai's novel, *Where Shall We Go This Summer?* (1975). Both Sita and Saru are faced with an identical dilemma in their lives. They are not their normal selves by any means. Their existential problems do not allow them rest or relief, and in utter helplessness they run away to their parent's homes, hoping against all hopes to get over the sense of frustration and alienation. Surely, both of them go out in search of 'self' or in quest of identity.

That Long Silence depicts Jaya as a torn 'self' or a split personality. Jaya is shown reflecting on what she was before her marriage and what she has become after it. Hers is a peculiar dilemma—'to be or not to be'. In the span of seventeen long years of married life, she is blessed with a son and a daughter. But her husband's corrupt practices at his Bombay office and the ensuing inquiries and Jaya's unredeemed domestic drudgery and tortuous confinement to the Dadar flat wreck her conjugal life. Adele King characterises these to fortunate developments as "odd misfits" and "petty bickerings over money" and "jealousy over affections".[15] Jaya's relations, as a consequence, with her man run into a rough weather, and they become cold towards each other observing an unbreakable 'long silence'. The trouble arises from Jaya's fitful anger, and she calls Mohan's mother a 'cook' (which she certainly was). Mohan has never expected this from his well-educated and well-cultured English-speaking wife, and he has always thought that anger makes "a woman unwomanly" (83). His dreams are now shattered, and he slumps into a long-drawn silence. This worries her too much, and she starts wondering whether "there is such a thing as one's self, intact and whole, waiting to be discovered" (69). Jaya is actually a victim of circumstances, of "an atmosphere of apathy and boredom".[16] She is an alienated 'self' longing for love and companionship. It is at the close of the novel that she moves towards the realising of her true 'self'. Thus, the search for self-discovery or the quest for identity forms a recurrent motif in Deshpande's fiction, and the dominant metaphors used in it strengthen the motif.

This is further borne out by the short story entitled "I Want..." wherein a good deal of self-searching or self-exploration is carried on. The story has a twenty-seven-year-old Alka as its protagonist. She is young and unmarried and subject to "the insolent stares, and the impertinent questions"[17] by the groom's party. She feels uneasiness, consternation and hopelessness, and broods: "The woman in me was outraged and protested. I crushed her. She had no place there. None at all."[18] She is terribly upset within, and remarks: "Sometimes I feel we are all doomed to be strangers to one another, forever sealed in separate glass jars we call 'self'."[19] What keeps Alka apart from the commonality of women is her strong sense of 'self' which she wants to preserve at all cost. In a mood of self-preservation, she says: "I had a shape and form I had to preserve. A self I had to treasure."[20] Evidently, she is a woman of self-consciousness, and wants to discover her integral personality. As for her marriage, she has little choice of her own; moreover, her parents are there to safeguard her interests. But being a thoughtful woman, she has her own desire to fulfil. Though she does not desire a husband having a four-figure salary or a car, she still wants a man who "hears my voice when I speak, who understands me even when I don't...."[21] At the close of the story, she accepts the reassurances of her Baba (who immediately reminds us of Sarita's Baba in *The Dark Holds No Terrors*). Clearly, Alka wishes to shed off the slough of despair and darkness and to emerge in a world of companionship and sunlight.

Thus, Shashi Deshpande has woven a delicate and subtle texture of her fictional world with a good deal of thought and dexterity. Though the metaphors used in her novels are not many, they powerfully highlight the dichotomy of human life, characterised by sorrow and joy, failure and success, death and life, alienation and attraction, thereby setting the scale of existence balanced and reasonable, though the scale sometimes does swing towards misery and anguish, death and destruction, hopelessness and helplessness. These metaphors also reveal that Shashi Deshpande's world, like Jane Austen's, is a small and closed one, where the novelist is definitely at home.

NOTES

1. Ingram Bywater, *Aristotle: On the Art of Poetry.* Oxford: Clarendon Press, 1967, 78.
2. C. Day Lewis, *The Poetic Image.* Cambridge University Press, 1955, 4.
3. J. Middleton Murry, "Metaphor", *Twentieth Century Poetry,* eds. G. Martin & P.N. Furbank, Walton Hall, Milton Keynes. The Open University Press, 1975, 28.
4. K.R. Srinivasa Iyengar describes Saru as "an unusual character... who defies her mother to become a doctor, defies her caste to marry outside, and defies social conventions by using Boozie to advance her career". *Indian Writing in English.* New Delhi: Sterling Publishers, 1984, 759.
5. Shashi Deshpande, *The Dark Holds No Terrors.* 1980; Delhi: Penguin India, 1990, 11. (Textual references to Shashi

Deshpande's novels, except their first occurrence, have been given parenthetically.)

6. *Ibid.*, *It Was Dark*. Calcutta: Writers Workshop, 1986, 23.
7. *Ibid.*, *If I Die Today*. New Delhi: Vikas Publishing House, 1982, 5.
8. *Ibid.*, *Come Up and Be Dead*. New Delhi: Vikas Publishing House, 1983, 8.
9. *Ibid.*, *The Binding Vine*. Delhi: Penguin India, 1993, 20.
10. *Ibid.*, *The Legacy*. Calcutta: Writers Workshop, 1977, 87.
11. *Ibid.*, 95.
12. *Ibid.*, *Roots and Shadows*. New Delhi: Orient Longman (Disha Books), 1983, 83.
13. Sarabjit Sandhu, *The Novels of Shashi Deshpande*. New Delhi: Prestige Books, 1990, 41.
14. Shashi Deshpande, *That Long Silence*. Delhi: Penguin India, 1989, 147.
15. Adele King, "Shashi Deshpande: Portraits of an Indian Woman," in *The New Indian Novel in English*, ed. Viney Kirpal. Delhi: Allied Publishers, 1990, 165-66.
16. Madhu Singh, "Intimate and Soul-searching Portrayals of Marriage", *Indian Book Chronicle* (July 1993), 22.
17. Shashi Deshpande, *The Miracle*. Calcutta: Writers Workshop, 1986, 36.
18. *Ibid.*, 37.
19. *Ibid.*, 36.
20. *Ibid.*, 37.
21. *Ibid.*, 42.

Index

A

Alther, Lisa, 119
Amur, G.S., 120
Aristotle, 129
Austen, Jane, 121, 139
  Pride and Prejudice, 21

B

Bachchan, A.K., 111-12
Banerjea, Juliette, 121
  Boyfriend, The, 121
Batty, Nancy Ellen, 33, 36-37
  Ring of Recollection, The, 36
Beauvoir, Simone de, 6, 67, 112
  Second Sex, The, 6
Bhagavad Gita, The, 43, 60, 72, 94, 124
Boswell, James, 109
Broadhurst, Thomas, 70
  Advice to Young Ladies...., 70
Buckingham, 67

C

Carvalho, Stanley, 113
Chambers, Jessie, 22
Chanda, Ho and Mathai, 35
Chandra, Suresh, 59-60, 92
Collins, Patricia Hill, 103
Cormack, 90
Christie, Agatha, 134
Culler, Jonathan, 83

D

Daruwalla, Keki N., 82
Das, B.K., 52, 58
Defoe, Daniel, 19, 51
Derrida, Jacques, 67
  Spurs: Nietzoche's Styles, 68
Desai, Anita, 24, 81, 85, 88, 91-92, 110, 124, 127, 137
  Cry, The Peacock, 50, 88, 92
  Where Shall We Go This Summer?, 85, 92, 124, 127, 137
  Fire on the Mountain, 24, 110
  Clear Light of Day, 81
De, Shobha, 93
  Socialite Evening, 93
Deshpande, Shashi, 1-3, 9-19, 21, 23-25, 27-28, 30-31, 33, 35-37, 39, 42, 45-46, 50-52, 56-57, 59-62, 65, 70, 72, 75, 78-87, 93-94, 98-99, 108-29, 131, 134-35, 138-39

Dark Holds No Terrors, The, 82, 95, 122, 126, 130-31, 135-36, 139
If I Die Today, 132, 134
Come Up and Be Dead, 132-34
Roots and Shadows, 28, 55, 81-83, 135
That Long Silence, 1-2, 6, 15, 21-23, 25-26, 28, 30-31, 36-37, 40, 42, 45, 55-56, 62, 65, 78, 89, 98, 108, 109-12, 114-15, 127, 135-37
Binding Vine, The, 82, 84, 87, 111, 134-35
Small Remedies, 28, 82, 113
Moving On, 28
Legacy and Other Stories, The, 121-22
It Was Dark, 123
It Was the Nightingale, 123
"The Miracle", 125
Dhar, T.N., 51
Dickens, Charles, 108
David Copperfield, 21
Dickman, Sue, 113
Dinesh, Kamini, 57
Dwivedi, A.N., 73

E

Eichenbaum, Boris, 24
Erikson, Erik, 94
Eysturoy, Annie O., 75

F

Fielding, Henry, 108
Formalism, 24-25
French, Marilyn, 118
Women's Room, 118
Freud, 93
Futehally, Shama, 47

G

Gandhi, Mahatma, 8
Gandhian, 123
Gandhism, 8
Globalization, 67
Gour, Rashmi, 23, 26-28

H

Halperin, John, 24-25
Theory of the Novel, 24-25
Hamilton, 42
Hardy, Thomas, 108
Heidegger, 67
Hemingway, Ernest, 22
Farewell to Arms, A, 22
Holm, Chandra, 37
Holmes, Janet, 69
Holmes, Sherlock, 134
Hough, Graham, 22
Hurston, Zola Neile, 101
Their Eyes Were Watching God, 101
Hussain, Yasmin, 33
Hyat, Pierre, 39

I

Ibsen, Henrik, 81
Doll's House, A, 81
Ivanic, Roz, 74
Writing and Identity, 74
Iyengar, K.R. Srinivasa, 121

J

Jacobson, Roman, 24
Jain, Jasbir, 34
Jain, Naresh, 113

Women in Indo-Anglian Fiction: Tradition and Modernity, 113
Jameson, Fredric, 38
Jong, Erica, 119

K

Kakkar, Sudhir, 34
Kapur, Manju, 24
Difficult Daughters, 24
Immigrants, The, 24
Kerr, David, 60
Khair, Tabish, 36
Gothic, Postcolonialism and Otherness, The, 36
King, Adele, 1, 46, 50, 73, 76, 127, 138
Kirpal, Viney, 87
Kishwar, Madhu, 30, 32
Krook, Dorothea, 28
"Intentions and Intentions", 28

L

Lauretis, Teresa de, 99
Lawrence, D.H., 22, 108
Sons and Lovers, 21-22, 108
Lawrence, Lydia, 22
Lessing, Doris, 92, 118
Four-Gated City, The, 92
Golden Notebook, The, 92
Lewis, C. Day, 129
Locke, 86
Second Treatise, 86

M

Mahabharata, The, 11, 51
Markandaya, Kamala, 80
Silence of Desire, A, 80
Marra, Meredith, 69
Maslow, Abraham, 94
Mehta, Gita, 82
Mehta, Rama, 24, 87, 110
Inside the Haveli, 24, 87, 110
Menon, Madhavi, 62
Milgram, Stanley, 78
Mills, Sara, 70
Minh-ha, Irinh T., 73
Moller, Alfred H., 92
Morrison, Toni, 104-05
Sula, 105
Song of Solemon, 105
Mukherjee, Minakshi, 39
Murry, Middleton, 129

N

Narasimhan, Raji, 121
Marriage of Bela, The, 121
New Society, 49
Nietzsche, 67
Nimbkar, Jai, 47
Joint Venture, A, 47

O

Ortege, 25

P

Pal, Adesh, 91
Palkar, Sarla, 46, 61
Paterman, Carole, 86
Plath, Sylvia, 106
Bell Jar, The, 106
Proust, Marcell, 98
Punter, David and Glennis Byron, 41
Gothic, The, 41
Puri, Jyoti, 34
Woman, Body, Desire in Postcolonial India, 34

R

Rajan, Rajeshwari Sunder, 70, 95
Rani, T. Ashoka, 59
Rao, Vimala Rama, 51
Riviere, Joan, 100
Robins, Elizabeth, 23, 45
Rushdie, Salman, 21
  Midnight's Children, 21

S

Sahgal, Nayantara, 82
  Rich Like Us, 82
Sandhu, Sarabjit, 50, 52, 136
Sartre, Jean-Paul, 88
Sedgwick, Eve Kosofsky, 37
  Coherence of Gothic Conventions, The, 37
Sharma, Anjana, 99
Sheshadri, Veena, 80
Shklovsky, Victor, 24
  "At as Technique", 24
Singh, Madhu, 47
Singh, Vinod K., 113
Sobti, Pragati, 74
Socrates, 124
Spencer, Herbert, 110
Spivak, Gayatri, 67
  "Can the Subaltern Speak?", 68
Sundarajan, Louise, 75-76
Suneel, Seema, 48

T

Tennyson, Lord, 83
Tomashersky, Boris, 24

V

Vicar of Wakefield, The, 21

W

Walsh, William, 28, 108
  Indian English Literature, 28
Woolf, Virginia, 118

Y

Yardi, Anjali, 53